To M[...]

ARE YOU S.A.N.E.

(Setting A New Example)

Changing Who You Are
by
Changing How You Think

Be the change!

Jonathan

JONATHAN Z. QUEEN

AS(KAR)
Publishing, LLC.

ISBN 10: 0-9773347-9-1
ISBN 13: 978-0-9773347-9-7

This book has been catalogued with the Library of Congress

Cover Photo by: Lou Lambert of Lupah Ent.
Cover design by: Laura Ravenhorst

Published by:
Asikari Publishing, LLC
PO Box 478
Lexington, VA 24450

www.asikaripublishing.com
www.myspace.com/asikari_publishing

ASIKAR)
Publishing, LLC.

DEDICATION

For you. Thank you for joining me on this journey. Let's change the world.

And for my brothers: JJ, Caron, James, Jeron and Jaalil. Because I believe in you and your ability to set a new example.

CONTENTS

CONTENTS
(Continued)

CONTENTS
(Continued)

Change will not come if we wait for some other person or some other time. We are the ones we've been waiting for. We are the change that we seek.

— Barack Obama, 44th President of the United States of America

I'm starting with the man in the mirror. I'm asking him to change his ways.

—'Man in the Mirror' by Michael Jackson

I WAS CRAZY

The unexamined life is not worth living.
— Socrates

First and foremost, please understand that mental illness is not the insanity I wish to confront here. I am very sensitive to the fact that mental illness is a psychosis; most often incurable and only managed marginally with medication. No! The insanity I wish to expose and confront is a disease that can be cured with change. It is the insanity once defined by the brilliant Albert Einstein as '*doing the same thing over and over again and expecting different results.*'

There lies the madness that leads to alcoholism, drug addiction, criminality, corruption, violence, promiscuity, and many more of the ills that plague our world today. When I talk about not being sane and when I use the word 'crazy' or insane I am referencing the Einstein definition and one's inability to change even when they recognize they are wrong.

S.A.N.E. is also an acronym for; **Setting A New Example**. My motive, my objective, my mission is to set a new example. I truly believe every living soul should make a conscious effort to set an example of righteousness not only for themselves but for everyone they come in contact with–from their closest family members to the strangers they meet in passing.

I am not a doctor or a professor. I do not have any college degrees or fancy letters at the end of my name. I definitely do not have all of the answers. So, who am I and what gives me the authority and the audacity to write about change and setting new examples?

I am the new example. And I make that powerful statement with a compatible mix of pride and humility. You see, I was crazy. I was ignorant and insane. I've spent over two-thirds of my life doing the same negative things over and over again. Although I am only a few years removed from my lunacy; my deeply embedded sickness, I now represent how powerful change can be when you are open to the challenge of accepting change in your life.

The authority comes from God. It is only by God's grace that I am alive today and able to share these words with you. He has given me the desire, responsibility and obligation to share with you my experiences; how I learned to take ownership of my thoughts and actions in order to feel the way *I want* to feel.

The audacity is based solely on the reality that I continue to triumph over my old nature and the life-threatening mentality that guided my decisions for such a substantial part of my existence. I spent many years of my life resisting change and refusing to listen to the positive voice screaming from my spirit to let go of the dangerous attitudes I had adopted. I can't help but speak on and testify about the goodness and glory of God and I will allow Him to use me in any way His wonderful purpose calls for.

I was crazy! Would you like to know how crazy I was? I went to prison three times in a four-year span. I was doing the same thing over and over again and expecting different results. I sold drugs–I was arrested–I went to jail. I got out... I sold drugs–I was arrested–I went to jail. I got out... I sold drugs–I was arrested... you get the picture. My last offense, which was my third felony, earned me the distinction of being labeled a career-criminal. I was sentenced to ten years in a federal prison. I was 23-years-old and I was crazy!

What made my sickness so severe is I had convinced myself, as well as others, that I was the most rational and logical person alive. I had also become adept at defending my insanity to those who had the courage to call me on it and point out when I was wrong. My denial was undeniable. I was a mess.

However, this book and the man I am today is an example of how wonderful God is. He took what the devil intended for bad and He made it good. My insanity, my craziness has now become my credibility. I not only have the tools to overcome 'thoughtless thinking' I also have the background to relate to those who still struggle with being sane.

Does that mean you should read this book? Well, let me expound on my life and you can decide for yourself.

I was raised in a single-parent home, the oldest of four brothers and one sister. My childhood was welfare and food stamps, hand me downs and evictions. We cooked Ramen Noodles with water heated up on the kerosene heater. I remember walking across town to my aunt's house with hand-written notes asking to borrow food and missing school because I had nothing to wear. If the topic is poverty, I can talk about that.

I left home and dropped out of school at the age of sixteen. I earned my GED the following year and spent a semester in community college. While in prison, I worked as a GED Tutor/ Educational Aide for over 80 percent of my incarceration. I taught men, young and old–who made thousands and sometimes millions of dollars in their criminal enterprises–how to read beyond a third grade level and do simple fractions. When it comes to the high school dropout rate and how it affects the crime rate or why our young people are choosing the streets over school, well, I can talk about that.

As a teen, I was a 'playa' (playboy) and I had a host of different girlfriends throughout my teenage years; sometimes two and three girlfriends at the same time. I fathered two children at the age of sixteen. They were born four months apart. I fathered another child six months later. At the age of 19, I had four children, not only out of wedlock, but also with two different women. So, if we are speaking about promiscuity and being a 'baby with babies,' or a 'dead beat' dad, I can talk about that.

I grew up in the golden era of Hip-Hop and witnessed the growth of a multi-billion dollar industry. I began rapping at the age of 11. I was a founding member of the R&B/Rap group Ace Duce. I've owned a record label, spent countless hours in recording studios, released albums/CDs, managed a night club, promoted concerts and toured throughout the east coast. I have also been incarcerated with men who truly believed their crimes were committed as a result of a song they had heard. If we are discussing the state of Hip-Hop or the power and influence of music in general; yes I can talk about that.

Both my parents were addicts. Alcohol, marijuana, 'pills,' cocaine, crack, heroin. I grew up in an environment where drinking and drugs were not only accepted but also encouraged. I began drinking at the age of fourteen and smoking marijuana at fifteen. I can clearly recall a time in my life when I 'needed' to drink and smoke a few 'blunts' in order to feel like myself. I truly believed that I functioned better when I was high. Although, my substance abuse is limited to alcohol and marijuana, I have spent years in classes and treatment programs with men and women who were addicted to every drug under the sun. From a heroin addict who lay in bed shaking and soiling himself for three days as he went through withdraw to a methamphetamine addict who claims he once stayed awake for 28 days. You want to discuss alcoholism and addiction? I can talk about that.

I was shop lifting, breaking into houses and cars at age thirteen; stealing cars at fourteen. I started selling drugs at fifteen. By the time I was 16, drug dealing had become my disillusioned career choice. I was in the streets 18 hours a day; selling drugs, getting high, and ducking the police. I later grew in my illegal profession and began travelling to other cities and states in an effort to supply drugs to other communities where the profits were greater. I also spent vast amounts of money on cars, clothes, food, women and entertainment. So, if the subject is criminality and the addiction to that lifestyle, I can talk about that.

I've spent over a thousand hours in drug and alcohol treatment. I've taken courses in criminal thinking errors and rational thinking. I've received cognitive therapy, counseling, education and instruction that would have cost the average person almost a quarter million dollars. I became the recipient of such a required rehabilitation because I was in prison. I have committed myself to giving as much as I have learned and remembered to any and all who need it now; and who would much rather receive it without having to go to prison.

Although, I was crazy, I am now a happily married, faithful husband. I am a very involved father. I am an ordained deacon at my church and a little league football coach. I am a published author, a motivational speaker, a poet, a playwright, a Government

Contract Manager, and the Vice-President of Asikari Publishing LLC. I haven't touched alcohol or drugs in over six years. Most importantly, I am a man of God. Yet, I am still a work in progress. Therefore, if the dissertation is about change and the continuous evolution thereof, well, I can talk about that.

Does that mean you should read this book? As I stated in the dedication, **this book is for you**. Even if you do not match the profiles I've mentioned or fall into any of the 'crazy' categories I've listed in my life experiences, this book is still for you. Even if you live a life free of madness and drama. You must ask yourself; "Am I living a life that sets a new example?"

Are you SANE? Are you doing your absolute best to provide those who are influenced by you an example that will guide them in the future? Whether you are a parent, an older sibling, an aunt or uncle, a supervisor, a friend, an author, athlete or entertainer. Are you setting a new example?

This book is not only a guide for those who need help, but also for those who want to give help. Those who want to understand why their loved one is 'crazy' and wants so desperately to help them become better. Please let me share with you. Take what you wish; what applies to you and pass the rest to someone who needs the rest. This book is part 'How To' and part 'Motivational,' yet it is all 'Inspiring.'

I will share with you pieces of my life experiences with an unbiased honesty. I've learned that a person is more receptive to feedback when they know their instructor/teacher or in this case, author, has been through similar situations. My transition was established by all of my life changes; therefore, I will often take you to the streets, to school, into treatment and into church.

I will tell it like it is and offer some much needed tough love/ real talk. My only request is that as you embark on this journey with me you become open to the undeniable reality that change is possible. That becoming sane is not only an opportunity, but also a responsibility.

As you open this book, I ask you to open your mind, your heart and your spirit. That you embrace the challenge of setting a new example and changing the world by changing your mind, one thought at a time.

Let's Go!!!

PART 1

THE 'DON'T BLAME ME' MENTALITY

Don't blame me. I was given this world
I didn't make it
— Tupac

The 'Don't Blame Me' mentality is like a disease. It is a self-inflicted sickness that allows a person to disassociate their actions with their consequences. This attitude takes such deep root within a person's nature, that they adopt a self-righteous defense of their behaviors and become disconnected to the responsibility of their actions.

Don't Blame Me! These are the words of the alcoholic who claims he drinks because his father drank. Don't Blame Me! The words of the bully who says he attacks because he was picked on when he was younger and the words of the pregnant teenager who claims she only slept with him because nobody ever told her she was beautiful. Don't Blame Me! The words of the gang banger who claims he only joined the gang because his older brother did and the words of the high school dropout who claims he left because he was too far behind.

"I come from a dysfunctional family. The school system was terrible. My parents didn't hug me enough. I was raised around

9

drug addicts and drug dealers. Everyone else was doing it. My neighborhood was rough. I did what I had to do to survive. It's not my fault! Don't Blame Me!"

I suffered greatly from the 'Don't Blame Me' mindset and those are only a few of the excuses I used to justify the poor decisions I've made in my life. Those bad decisions led to a criminal lifestyle that culminated in a third felony conviction and a ten-year prison sentence.

"I sold drugs in order to provide a better life for my children." That is what I told myself. In my insanity, that is what I believed. I was convinced that buying my one-year old daughter an 18 karat gold ID bracelet and my eight-month old son a pair of Nike Air Jordans, could make up for the no-name sneakers and hand-me-down clothes I wore as a child. Yet, in my pursuit to gain material things through illegal means, I denied my children the main thing I so desperately desired as a child–time spent with their father.

I have since learned that I did have other options and that I chose to take a negative path because I wanted things fast and easy and on my terms. I was selfish, arrogant and ignorant. I was utterly vicious. I was crazy! And I had the audacity to ask if you could blame me?

I convinced myself that if I didn't 'go hard,' I wouldn't make it. I believed the whole world was against me and I used those feelings to excuse my insane behavior. I told myself that somebody owed me something for the horrible life I had.

It became easy for me to take from others; to hurt others. There were times when I was younger that I was hungry; times when I was cold or didn't have nice clothes to wear. I endured some difficult times, so I refused to feel bad about taking money from the mother or father of a child or children who may have to deal with the same hunger, cold and embarrassment I dealt with. On the rare occasions when my true sensitivity did surface and I felt some type of guilt, I turned to drugs and alcohol to numb me. I didn't want to feel. I didn't want to be soft.

Does a Real Man Cry?

I share with many a poem I wrote, entitled 'Shine.' In the poem, I reflect back to my Sunday School days and how I once gave one of my only two quarters to a friend of mine so that he would have money for the offering. I have often been asked how that kind and caring boy became a manipulative, street drug-dealing criminal. The answer is sad in its simplicity. I became a follower instead of the leader God called me to be.

When someone told me it was weak to give hugs, I followed. When they said it was soft to show compassion, I followed. They told me not to care, and if I did, to hide it as best as I could and I followed. I brought into the myth and the stereotype that says being a man means being tough. The same ignorance we continue to pass down to our young men today.

We tell them a real man doesn't cry. A real man doesn't show affection to his family, friends or even his children. A real man doesn't wash dishes or clothes. A real man will fight to prove his point or earn the respect he desires. A real man drinks hard liquor without scrunching his face. A real man doesn't work a nine-to-five. A real man hustles so that he can beat the system. A real man goes to prison at least once. A real man has more than one girlfriend and keeps his girlfriends in check even if that means hitting them every now and then.

These are the adages and creeds our young men are being reared under. We have a generation of callous, desensitized young men. No one is hugging these kids or telling them they love them. We are failing to encourage them to become more than what they hear in some of the rap songs and see in those sadistic video games. These kids see the same horrible situations time after time. They don't see any change and they begin to believe their lot in life is predestined. It is time for us to make some changes and represent with complete confidence what it truly means to be a real man.

A real man takes full responsibility for his actions; he stands up to ignorance and isn't afraid to admit when he is wrong. A real man finds joy, comfort and peace in the arms of true love and does not need a bunch of different women calling him Boo, Baby, or Daddy in order to boost his self-esteem. A real man recognizes and cherishes the beauty, softness and life creating nature of women; he would never raise a hand to hurt, injure or destroy it or her.

A real man hugs his children and holds them in his arms whether they are happy or sad, proud or disappointed, confident or afraid. He looks them in their eyes and tells them he loves them whether they are 8 months old, 8 years old or 18 years old. A real man knows his responsibility is to represent the image of God and be a loving, nurturing, and guiding rock to his family.

A real man knows the value of hard work and would much rather earn something to call his own than take something that could be taken away from him at anytime. A real man values freedom more than temporary wealth, he appreciates time with his family more than time running the streets or playing games. A real man is a man who sees the unconstructive course our world is on and he sets a new example.

CONDITIONS AND COGNITIONS

**Life is 10 percent what happens to us and
90 percent how we respond to it.
—Albert M Wills, Jr.**

Before I go deeper, let me be clear. I do recognize the relationship between conditions and cognitions. In layman terms, I know that how and where we are raised will influence and impact how we think. My goal here is to help you recognize that although your experiences and circumstances (conditions) can have a powerful impact on how you view the world and even more importantly how you see yourself, it does not have to have the power to determine how you think and believe (cognitions). **Let's go into treatment.**

Tyra was raised in an abusive home. Either her mother, Elaine was too in love or too afraid to leave the man who blackened her eye and bloodied her lip at least once a week. Tyra has vivid memories of watching this man, who she called Uncle Mack, punch her mother in the face and then kick her over and over again as she laid on the ground screaming, "I love you!" while trying in vain to protect her face from his size 12 work-boots.

Tyra is now a recovering drug addict and ex-prostitute. She has two children in foster care. She has very little self-esteem and believes she can tell how much a man loves her only by how hard he hits her.

Tara is Tyra's sister. She is only one year younger than Tyra. Tara was raised in the same house and witnessed the same pattern of incessant abuse. She sadly recalls how, at age 11, she cried herself to sleep almost every night for an entire year.

Today, Tara is a Probation Officer with a Bachelor's Degree in Criminal Justice. She is very outspoken and is a staunch supporter of women's rights. She is happily married to a good man, who she states, "would apologize profusely if he even thought about raising his hand to me."

Like Tyra and Tara, who suffered through the exact same conditions, you have the option and the God-given authority to choose how you allow your conditions to affect your cognitions. You do not have to become a victim of the circumstances that were beyond your control. You become the victor by using every hurt and pain, every scratch and scar as a motivator to do and think differently.

No matter what our conditions we always have the power of choice. We can choose to excel in spite of our conditions. That is what we should endeavor to do. I could write about numerous cases where the conditions were identical and because the cognitions were different, the results were different. I know biological brothers who are cop and convict; drug dealer and Marine; dead beat dad and devoted father.

I could talk about sisters who are alcoholic and Pastor; prisoner and lawyer; stripper and small business owner. It boils down to choice and as we go deeper, we will identify some strategies for making good choices, but first let us continue to clean out the wound that represents the lack of accountability.

Denial (A River in Africa)

"How many of you know what denial is?"

When I was in treatment my favorite response to that question was, "Da Nile? That's a river in Africa, right?"

My classmates and I thought it was funny until our treatment counselor flipped it on us and said, "Actually it's an acronym for; *Don't Even kNow I Am Lying*." I eventually learned that denial is the root of the 'Don't Blame Me' mentality.

Sigmund Freud defines denial as: *Ignoring or refusing to believe an unpleasant reality.* Denial develops defense mechanisms that block us from admitting we have a problem. We refuse to recognize there is a need for help. Denial is the problem that says we have no problem. When we do see a problem, we blame other people or external things that we say we have no control over.

"I am doing these terrible things because of everything and everyone except me." When faced with the irrefutable damages of our actions, denial prevents us from being accountable and making amends.

If your first instinct or mental reflex is to avoid blame at all costs, you have already committed yourself to a lifestyle of irresponsibility. You must become self accountable in order to become Sane. **Self Accountable No Excuses** is another acronym for SANE and it is the counter punch to the many defenses we use to support our denial. A few of which are:

Rationalizing–is when we make excuses for what we are doing wrong. "I drink because I'm stressed out."

Minimizing–is when we make it seem like our actions aren't a big deal. "I only hit her once."

Generalizing–is when we say something as a general truth and that it applies to all things and all people. "I sell drugs because everybody else does."

Switching–is when we switch the focus to someone or something else when confronted. "Why are *you* always so uptight? What's wrong with *you*?"

There are many more and they all guarantee the same result– a failure to address the real problem. As it is with alcoholism, addiction and gambling, the first way to overcome the problem is to admit you have one. This is your symbolic first step and it is definitely the most difficult. You have to look at yourself with complete honesty. You have to admit you are aware of the disease and therefore acknowledge the need for medicine. In addition, when you make a poor choice or bad decision you own up to it or like I tell my children, "you don't make excuses; you make changes."

WHAT DID YOU DO

There are often times when I have to settle a dispute between my children and it amazes me how amusing it becomes when I insist that they only speak in relation to *their* actions. The fun comes with one simple question: What did you do? Allow me to give you a visual.

I hear yelling coming from my 13-year-old daughter's bedroom. "Get out of my room!" Then I hear something less decipherable from my 7-year-old son.

"No! I said get out!" She yells again.

My son mentions something about Zach and Cody being in Corey's House with Sponge Bob Square Pants. Well, something like that.

"If you don't get out right now, I'm going to—"

She doesn't finish with the threat because she decides to carry it out. I hear a thump, a scream, a door slam and then running feet. I meet them in the dining room where they both shout out one of my favorite words in the English language, "Daddy!" However, it comes out in a tone that reminds me of fingernails scraping across a chalkboard.

My cognitive treatment has taught me to be accountable by always beginning with what I did and then identifying what I could have done differently. So, instead of asking what happened, I look at my son who is grimacing and holding his arm; then to my daughter who is breathing hard through flared nostrils. I ask her, what did you do?

"Nothing," she says indignantly. "He just came in my room without knocking and then he wouldn't leave when I told him to."

"Uh uhn," he counters. "She hit me in my arm with the remote control."

"He kicked me."

"You hit me first."

"Did not!"

"Did too!"

"Did not!"

"Did too!"

I let them go back and forth for a few "did not, did too's." I then give my son a chance to be the better man. What did **YOU** do? I emphasize. He actually thinks for a second and then uses one of his new big words.

"*Actually*, she told me I could watch TV in her room then she tried to change her mind—"

"No, you barged up in my room without knocking. I could have been getting dressed."

"Ain't nobody trying to look at you get dressed, Ugly."

I look at them. They look at me. I tell them to go to their rooms; no TV, phone, PSP, iPod or anything until they are ready to tell me what they take responsibility for. My daughter catches on first.

She sighs, "I yelled at him and I did tap him on the arm with the remote."

And what could you have done differently, I inquire.

"I could have asked him politely to leave and I shouldn't have put my hands on him," she says while staring at the floor.

"Actually, you used the remote, not your hands," he says matter of factly. My daughter rolls her eyes as if to say he is such a brat. I ask him, what did he do?

"Well, I didn't knock on the door, I stuck my tongue out at her, I didn't leave when she told me to and I kicked her in the shin. But that's all."

And what could you have done differently?

"I should have knocked on her door and I should have kept my feet to myself."

They apologize to each other and more importantly, they continue to learn how to acknowledge their role in the conflict. The goal is for them to reach the point where they no longer give power to someone else to dictate their thoughts, feelings or actions.

This approach is great for most conflict resolution. Husbands and wives vent to their friends about how their spouse wracks their nerves, but imagine if you took the time to think of the things you do which may frustrate your spouse. What did you do? Your husband forgot to hang up his coat... Again. But you walked around the grocery store three times and still forgot something that your husband went back to get. What did you do? Your wife packed your lunch but forgot your drink, but it was you who didn't put a new roll of toilet paper on the holder.

What did you do? I bring up these minor issues because when the fight occurs, these are the issues that swim underneath the surface and if you take the time to focus on what you did or didn't do it eliminates the rumination that provokes finger pointing and fuels a blow up.

When a person has to put the focus on what he/she is responsible for it helps them work on the part of the problem that is in their power to change. This power teaches them how to recognize they are ultimately responsible for their choices, thus they will be open for solutions even when apologies are called for and consequences are handed out.

The Falseness of Feelings

**No one can make you feel inferior
without your consent.
—Eleanor Roosevelt**

"Now, see what **You made** me do!" "**You make** me treat you this way!" "**You make** me **feel** like…"

One of the most powerful truths I have learned is, no one can make you do or feel anything you don't want to do or feel or as the seniors say, "I don't see anybody holding a gun to your head." You have to recognize your power to choose how you want to think and feel.

Make no mistake about it; your feelings can be false, especially if they are not based on rational thoughts. Think about the times when you woke up and said to yourself, "I feel awful. There is no way I can make it to work today." But you did get up and you made it, even though your 'feelings' said otherwise.

To go even deeper, remember how you felt you were 'so in love' at the ripe old age of fifteen. How you felt you couldn't live without that special someone. Yet, you broke up three weeks later and the world did not end. Actually, that particular falseness of feelings can take affect when your 15, 25 or 45 years old. My point is you have to be aware of the relationship between your thoughts and your feelings as well as the power you have to control both.

Someone calls you ugly or says you are not good for anything. Do you believe them? Do you accept that as your truth? Do you give that person the power to define who you are or will become? No! You do not! Your feelings are based on what **you** believe; what you think, so if you believe you are beautiful then you will feel beautiful and if you believe you are worthy and valuable, you will feel worthy and valuable.

It is up to you to determine how you feel about yourself and for those times when you forget how to think thoughts that are in tune with how you want to feel, let me show you a proven method that will lead to you changing how you feel by changing how you think.

Easy as ABC

**The only person you are destined to
become is the person you decide to be.
—Ralph Waldo Emerson**

Here is the scenario: You are driving around the parking lot of a crowded grocery store. As you round the bend, you see a big SUV halfway in/out of a spot only a few feet from the door. You stop and wait to see if they are pulling out. They are. You smile and think how lucky you are. The SUV pulls out and you back up a little so it can get around you. Then out of nowhere, a little sports car pulls into the spot. You lean on the horn in anger; you curse and actually consider getting out and confronting the spot stealer.

Does this sound familiar? Has it ever happened to you? Did it make you crazy? How did you handle it? Let us break down the sane way to handle situations like this.

It is known as the ABC's of Rational Self Analysis and it is a part of the Rational Emotive Behavior Therapy (REBT) created by Albert Ellis. Please note that to be sane one must also be rational. Let us go deeper.

The A is the Activating event. The B is the Beliefs; the thoughts we have and what our self-talk is. The C is the Consequences; how we feel and what we do. In the above scenario, we would write it out like this.

A (Activating Event) Someone stole my parking space.

B (Beliefs) They saw me here. That is my spot. Stupid Bastard! I should key their car.

C (Consequence) You feel angry. You pull off in a rage and hit a parked car.

Of course, a very important D follows the ABCs. Once you can honestly analyze what you believe the event consisted of you can take the courageous step to D–Dispute it. You must re-examine the entire event and it is not easy. You have to step away from the 'Don't Blame Me/Denial' mind-set and identify where you were wrong. The beautiful part is, after enough practice, this process will take only seconds and you will have the satisfaction of recognizing how much control you truly have over your feelings and actions.

In describing the scenario above, I embellished and exaggerated a little, as many of us do when telling our side of the story. When I listed the (A), I worded it as an accusation: *Someone stole my spot.* That alone will lead to negative thoughts and actions. Understand that, although the actual event is based on one's perception, it can most often be identified by certain facts. Thus, A is the easiest component to change because we simply have to state the facts of what happened. How does this sound?

A. A car pulled into the parking spot I was waiting for.

C. *Then I got mad and pulled off so fast I hit another car.*

Many of us would jump to (C) because that is usually how we perceive the sequence of events. If someone asked you why you are so angry, your answer would be along the lines of "because someone took my parking spot." What you fail to understand is that when you equate your feelings and your behavior to the activating event then you give your power to something outside of your control.

This is why it is so important to be aware of our self-talk. Our thoughts and our beliefs are truly ours and we have the power to change them when needed. Let's break B down thought by thought.

B - *(Beliefs) They saw me here.* Are you absolutely sure, they saw you? Think about it, you didn't see them. The correct self-talk could be–*Maybe they didn't see me here waiting.*

That is my spot. Is the spot really yours? Do you own that particular piece of land? You really can't say for sure if you were even there first. The correct self-talk could be–*I don't own any of these spaces and they may have been here first, waiting on the other side.*

Stupid Bastard! Name-calling and put-downs are defense mechanisms we use to help us stay angry. You have no idea how intelligent that person may be or what their parents marital status was at their birth. The correct self-talk could be–*I don't know them and I don't think they know me. It's not personal.*

I should key their car. This is where the thoughts become dangerous. You have allowed your anger to reach the point where you are considering doing something criminal, something crazy. The correct self-talk could be–*It is not that serious. I can find another spot.*

C - *(*Consequence) You feel less angry. You pull out calmly and find another spot within 45 seconds. After shopping for an hour, you no longer think about the "stolen" parking spot. Whereas, the bill to fix your car and the one you hit, along with the increase in your car insurance, will have you ruminating about that parking spot for a very long time.

I can attest to how successful the ABCs are in dealing with stress causing situations. I have learned to check my self-talk (beliefs) as soon as I feel the warning signs from my body. When my jaw clenches and my fists ball up or I feel my heart beat speeding up; I instantly recognize I am allowing the situation to affect me in a negative way. I've learned from my past experiences that I don't make good decisions when I feel hostile or aggressive. So, I go back in. I use that 'safe code' when I start feeling angry. *Go back in*. I see where the error is, change the thinking and change how I feel.

Does it work all of the time? Of course not. My wife and children could speak on the many times I forgot to *ABC* my attitude before responding to something they said or done. It takes time to learn and I am still a work in progress. Overall, the more you become accustomed to rational self-analysis the better you will be at handling conflict and adversity; the better you will become at setting a new example.

Speaking of examples, here are a few more to show you how diverse the ABCs are in altering one's attitude.

The Parent:

A. (Activating Event) My clumsy daughter spilled juice all over the dining room table.

B. (Beliefs) She's always messing up. She's such a klutz. Now I have to clean this up and *My* food is going to get cold. I could just scream.

C. (Consequence) You feel angry. You scream at your daughter, who cries as you storm off to get a towel for the table.

Dispute it:

A. (Activating Event) My 7-year-old daughter spilled her juice on the dining room table.

B. (Beliefs) It was an accident. It doesn't happen often. This is an opportunity for me to teach her about cleaning up after herself. I can heat our food up if it gets cold.

C. (Consequence) You feel calm instead of angry. Your daughter helps you clean up and you still enjoy a nice dinner.

The Teen

A. (Activating Event) Jay is trying to get me to smoke a cigarette.

B. (Beliefs) All of them smoke. I'll be considered cool if I smoke too. One cigarette won't hurt me. My parents will never find out.

C. (Consequence) You feel nervous and stressed out. You take a puff on the cigarette and choke. Jay laughs at you.

Dispute it:
A. (Activating Event) Jay offered me a cigarette.

B. (Beliefs) Everyone doesn't smoke. Smoking won't make me cool. One cigarette is one too many. I don't want to disappoint my parents.

C. (Consequence) You feel confident not stressed or scared. You say no and feel proud.

Some of you are reading this and saying to yourself, "That ABC stuff is corny. Jonathan Queen is tripping." I said the same thing and I can relate to your hesitation. But you're already here. You've opened the book and read this far. I assure you by the time we reach the end of this new journey you will have learned a few things that just might help you change your life or the life of someone you care about.

SANE Challenge

It is important that you come to terms with the part you played in the mess you made. You must let go of the 'Don't Blame Me' mentality and adhere to the other meaning for SANE (Self Accountable No Excuses)

1. Here is where you begin. Simply go somewhere you can

be alone with a mirror. Look into the mirror and stare into your own eyes. Stare until you see beyond your facial features. Look past the color of your eyes and peer into the windows of your soul. When you see past the image and recognize the real you; apologize to yourself. Apologize for every hurt you have caused yourself and others. Accept responsibility for your thoughts and actions; positive and negative.

Then forgive yourself. Let it go. Release the burdens and baggage that has blocked your growth. Gaze into your eyes and see who you were, who you are, and who you want to become. Stare until the tears come, stare until you see the power within you to become the change you desire to see. Open your mind, your heart and your spirit. Now say to yourself, **"I am free!"**

2. Take a note pad or composition book and write out a few Rational Self Analysis ABCs. Go through your day, pick out the times where you know you could have made better decisions, and write it out. You don't have to share it with anyone or tell anyone what you are doing. Just try it and see if you develop an awareness of how possible it is to change how you see a situation and how you react to it. Try it for a few days and when you see it is working, continue to write them in your book until you are able to do them in your head while the activating event is happening.

PART 2

PERSONAL PRISONS

***For no chains have kept me 'cept that which
was forged by my own hands***
—Unknown

Dear Mr. Queen,

*Peace, hope, joy, patience, and most of all love! I pray you
are reading this with an open mind and calm spirit, but knowing
you, if you are reading this it is because you are worried, anxious
or scared. It's okay, just take a deep breath and travel with me
down memory lane.*

*First, let's talk about time. 8 years, 11 months and 2 ½ weeks.
Or 3,271 days. Or 78,504 hours. Or 4,710,240 minutes. That is
how long you've spent in prison. Not including the 18 months
you served for your first two felonies. Your children grew from
Chuck-E-Cheese lovers to mature teenagers with driver licenses,
money problems and significant others. And you missed it all. You
were a stranger who wrote letters and called once in a while. You
almost became a grandfather and your son cursed and used the
N-word like it was nothing. You missed birthdays, Christmases
and first dates. You weren't there to talk to them about drugs,
alcohol and sex. Two of your children called you by your street
name Ace, not Dad or Father because you were neither.*

Remember how helpless you felt on the visit at Loretto when your son and daughter fought and cried for two days in a row, because that was the only way they could express their anger at you for leaving them... again. Remember the bitter letters from your oldest and how she constantly asked you why you weren't there when she needed you the most. Your children were crying out for you while you made jailhouse wine, smoked weed and ran gambling tickets. Remember how it felt being in the 'hole' for three months and how you broke down that night Jazmine sang to you over the phone.

Remember the tension and fear you felt when you were transferred to a higher security prison. Remember the drama. The fights. The stabbings. Remember your cellie, who was hit with a combination lock, and had to get 147 stitches in his head.

Let's talk about loss. Your grandmother passed when you were only a week into your Fed time. Remember the pain you felt when you were told you couldn't attend her funeral; the tears in your eyes as you wrote her poem. Your father died and you had spent most of his last years being angry with him. You couldn't even shed a tear for him at his service. Have you cried yet? Patience died. Dawn passed. Countless others, who you weren't even aware of, are no longer there.

Let's talk about change. Are you still trying to rescue everyone? Are you mistaking your wants for needs and chasing both? Are you being a father? A real father; who knows his time is his greatest gift. Are you recognizing your priorities or still trying to run everything? Are you being objective? Do you still demand things be done your way or not at all?

Are you respecting your vows? Do you remember the painful

visits with your wife when she had tears falling freely because of something that was said or done by a guard or you? Do you still appreciate the love and support she showed you for the last 5 years of your sentence? Have you kept your promises to her? Do you continue to love like you've never been hurt and like tomorrow may not come?

Jonathan Zaki Queen, you are a talented, intelligent, loving and gifted man. You are a light of God and every second of those 4.7 million minutes you spent in prison is a testimony of how much God loves you. The devil could have killed you when he had you, but God's plan is the best plan. So, whatever you're going through right now, you better shake it off, because it's not worth it. Look around you and see the love—not the chaos—and know that you have made it through much worse.

I sit here writing this letter to you, looking into the future. And I'm proud, because I know you are the man who pulls this letter out even when nothing is wrong. You pull it out simply because you don't want to ever go back—to prison or the old you. Hold your head up and if you don't remember anything else, remember that you are always that little boy who said he would shine.

Love,
Self

I wrote that letter on October 29, 2006 at 11:32 PM—my last night in prison. I pull it out every now and then; sometimes I *need* the reminder and other times I simply want to remember. I have gained so much from my prison experience and those lessons have become a constant point of reference for my teaching.

I've grown to realize the brick walls, barbed-wire fences and cell doors that held me in for so many years, represent only one of the many prisons I've spent time in. I use the prison 'cell' analogy because it is the most obvious and visual symbol of lost liberty. It is the universal understanding of forfeited freedom. Ah, but prison comes in so many forms.

You may have never had any dealings with the law or spent a day in jail. Still, you have become a prisoner. The alcoholic and drug addict are prisoners to their addiction. The woman who stays in a relationship ruled by domestic violence is a prisoner to abuse. The teenager who hates life and contemplates suicide is a prisoner to depression.

We become prisoners to gambling, sex and pornography. We are incarcerated by image, greed, worry and self-doubt. We create these personal prisons then become malicious wardens over ourselves. We deny ourselves the freedom to live better and like institutionalized felons, we adapt and accept our self-imposed confinement as natural.

Do you want to be free? As the quote mentions, your hands have forged the chains that bind you. Therefore, you have the power, the key to open the door to your prison. Unlike the slogan that marks the sacrifices of our military soldiers, this freedom *is* free.

If you have gained the strength to admit you have a problem, whether it be drugs, alcohol, criminal behavior, depression, or what you may consider only a vice; such as smoking cigarettes or eating unhealthy. If you have that awareness, then you are now prepared to confront your personal prison and demand an early release.

A Healthy Escape

I thought I was smart. I remember my mother asking me why I was trying to be like my so-called friends. She said, "If your friends jumped off a bridge would you jump too?"

I stared at her and after a brief pause I answered, "Yeah, I would. If that was the only way out, I would jump too."

I know there are many of you, young and old, reading this book and relating to that attitude. It's that 'do-or-die-me-against-the-world' attitude that helps us justify not making the right decisions. Yeah, you want out, but what is your perception of out? Just as there are many forms of prison, there are many ways out. You must first realize that everywhere you go–there you are. You will carry your prison with you until you decide to take hold of your freedom. Until you decide to get out.

Getting out or leaving does not always have to be a physical act. I was able to escape the harsh concrete reality of my 10 by 12-prison cell many times simply by picking up a book. I read and escaped. Not the type of escape that would lead to a nervous life of looking over my shoulder or even worse–more time in prison. No, it was a healthy escape that enabled me to start thinking and planning to become a better person.

It was the same escape I witnessed my mother accomplish when she curled up on a worn down couch in a living room heated by a kerosene heater; in a house that was three months past due on rent, gas and electricity. Poverty was a small part of her personal prison. Books were her escape.

I watched my mother read book after book and she would laugh out loud or cry big tears. I would call out "Mom!" over and over again and she would continue reading, oblivious to my complaint that my little brother called me a name or that the hot dogs were done cooking.

Those books were freedom to her. She escaped into a world of Harlequin romances where the men rescued and loved their women instead of using them and leaving them. I didn't understand it as a child, but when I found myself in my prison, I too turned to books for escape. I picked up books of fiction that took me to new worlds and different times. I explored ancient civilizations and different cultures. I slipped into a partnership with the protagonist and I read with the courage that *we* would overcome whatever challenges the plot threw at us.

I picked up non-fiction books that taught me how to do many new things. Books that enlightened me and helped me see things from a different light. I read autobiographies by people who had been in worse situations than mine; people who had survived and overcome odds too hard to make up. I read books that gave me hope. So, for those of you who believe you are a product of your environment and that you have no way out, let me emphatically tell you, there is always a way out.

The Foundations of the Prison Were Shaken

It is only fitting that since I am on the subject of books being an escape, I acknowledge the Book that truly set me free–The Holy Bible. I once read the Bible from beginning to end. I'm talking Genesis 1 to Revelation 22:21. I even read those long, hard to pronounce genealogies and the detailed laws of the Old Testament.

I have gone from merely reading the words to having a relationship with the Author and could point out numerous scriptures to confirm God's desire for us to be free. From his gift of free will to Him giving us Jesus so that we could be free from sin. Instead, I encourage you to take some time with an open mind and open up that great book of God's word and see what precious freedom awaits you. As a matter of fact, walk with me for a minute; this is too good not to share. **Let's go to church**!

And when they had laid many stripes upon them, they cast them into prison, charging the jailor to keep them safely: Who, having received such a charge, thrust them into the inner prison, and made their feet fast in the stocks. And at midnight Paul and Silas prayed, and sang praises unto God: and the prisoners heard them. And suddenly there was a great earthquake, so that the foundations of the prison were shaken: and immediately all the doors were opened, and every one's bands were loosed. And the keeper of the prison awaking out of his sleep, and seeing the prison doors open, he drew out his sword, and would have killed himself, supposing that the prisoners had been fled. But Paul cried with a loud voice, saying, Do thyself no harm: for we are all here.

Acts 16: 23-28

Paul and Silas were in (the inner prison) the 'hole.' How many of you know about the 'hole,' that inner prison? The hole is where you have even less space to move; where you are cut off from the rest of the population. It is a place of solitude and isolation. The corner your mind takes shelter in when you refuse to leave your personal prison. It is a dark and lonely place, where the sound of your own voice can startle you. The inner prison is a hell to some and a sanctuary for others. As we witness with Paul and Silas, it can also become the place for liberty.

Their feet were (fast in the stocks). They couldn't move. Recognize their freedom did not require movement or some vast amount of exerted energy. No, they prayed, they sang, and (the foundations of the prison were shaken). How powerful is that? We have a God who can shake the foundations of any prison we create. There is no depression, no addiction, no self imposed sanction too big for our God to break down and shake loose the rooted, long established ground work; the very core we spend so much of our time building up and fortifying with our fear and ignorance. He sends an earthquake; an awakening that shakes those beliefs and opens up doors.

Now, here is the part that warrants the big smile. The cuffs and shackles came off, the doors were open, yet they did not have to take a single step to realize they were free. Paul and Silas knew they were free even before they started singing. That was the reason for their praise. We must first believe in and acknowledge the choice to be free. Before the doors open, before the cuffs and shackles come off, we must accept freedom.

The passage states the keeper of the prison awakened from his sleep. Allow me to digress into another metaphorical analogy. Who is the keeper of your personal prison? Yes, it is you. (and seeing the prison doors open, he drew out his sword and would have killed himself). Meditate on that. Think about how resistant we are to being free. Many of us would rather die than change. Liberty or death and in our sickness we would choose death.

Oh, what a mighty God we serve. For even as our old prisoner/jailer self stares at our new open-door-free-self and that inner war begins and we contemplate death as an answer to this new path in front of us; God steps in and says, do no harm. We are still here. We are free, yet still in the environment that held our chains. We become the new example of freedom for those who are still in their bonds. We show how you can be free no matter what your outer circumstances reflect.

Still inside the prison serving time, but free. Still living in a neighborhood plagued with drugs and violence, but free. Raising three kids alone, but free. In school wearing the same jeans we wore yesterday, but free. In the hospital racked with pain from withdrawal, but free.

If you allow yourself to believe in the power, mercy and grace of God, I assure you that no matter what your situation or circumstance, you can simply be still, pray and sing songs of praise while your prison doors fly open granting you a freedom that doesn't even require a step. **Let's go to the streets!**

Kicking the Door In

It was the spring of 1993. My two-year-old son was living with me in a lavishly decorated apartment that sat directly across the street from an elementary school. I was dating at least four different girls, going to community college and directing a play for the high school my sister attended. I was drinking, smoking weed, partying at home and at nightclubs. Arrested less than six months ago and out on bail, I was still selling drugs, sometimes out of my apartment while my son was there. I was crazy!

My son had unplugged my waterbed heater earlier that day and the bed had become too cold to sleep in. My son and I fell asleep in the living room in front of the TV. It was a little after six in the am; The Harrisburg Police Department led by detectives from the Drug Task Force Unit kicked in my door with a search and seizure warrant. All I heard was the loud crash and when I looked up, I saw dark figures aiming guns and flashlights.

My son jumped up in fear and started to run for the bedroom or bathroom or anywhere away from all of the commotion. One of the police officers yelled, "Don't move!" but my son kept going. I reached out for him while at the same time screaming, "He's just a baby!" I pulled him close to me to shield him from any incoming bullets. By God's grace, the cop did not fire his gun.

Don't misconstrue my actions as some type of hood heroics. It was a natural instinct to try to protect my child from immediate danger. 'Self Accountable No Excuses' tells me it was I who placed my son in that danger. I exposed my son to drug dealers and addicts who I allowed to bring guns into my apartment. I gave the police the cause to kick in my door.

I was arrested in front of my son, who tried his best to squeeze into my arms underneath the handcuffs. The confusion and hurt of that day stayed with him for many years. I remember walking him to school when he was five years old and how he grabbed my hand, pulled me and implored me to run because he heard sirens in the distance. I wasn't doing anything wrong, but my son felt it necessary for us to run before the police got there. My actions scarred him emotionally and he would spend many years trying to squeeze between the handcuffs I kept between us.

I would spend one year in a state prison and 6 months in a county jail. Two years after my release, the cops kicked in my door again. This time, my state parole officer, police officers from three townships and the FBI accompanied them. I was convicted for a third felony, labeled a 'career criminal' and sentenced to 120 months in a Federal Correctional Institution.

Let us fast forward to the winter of 2001. I was still crazy. I was spending time in the hole of my first federal prison as a result of me running gambling tickets. I was in a cell for 23 hours a day and allowed one phone call every 30 days. With my first phone call, I tried desperately to remember the phone numbers of family and friends. My phone book was in the box of property I wasn't permitted to have while in the hole. I could remember only a handful of numbers and there was no answer at any of them.

I finally called my children's mother and spoke to my 8-year-old daughter. She was about to perform in a Christmas recital and was so excited about the solo she would be singing. I was smiling from ear to ear as I listened to her talk a mile-a-minute about how great the program is going to be. I asked her what she was going to sing and she answered, '*Joy to the World.*' Before I could ask, she offered to sing it to me over the phone.

And sing she did. Over and over. Every time she finished I would ask her to sing it again and she spent 10 minutes of that 15-minute-call singing *Joy to the World* to her absent father, who at that time, felt no joy in the world.

The poignancy of this story stems from a similar situation from a few years earlier. My daughter was doing something with either singing or dancing. Please forgive me, but the guilt I felt has blocked some of the details. The main part is she wanted me to go and she was at an age where she didn't understand why I couldn't. She begged me while holding back tears. She even asked if the prison would just let me out for a few hours and that she would promise them to bring me back. It was that important to her for me to be there. And because of my poor decisions she had to suffer my absence for that event and for so many other occasions.

What made the 'Joy to the World' phone call so painful is she neither asked nor expected me to be there. That is what broke me. My child, my baby had accepted that I would not be a part of the most important times of her life and she seemed to be okay with it. When we hung up the phone, I sat there and after a small fight with my false image, I let go and I cried like a baby. I had been doing things my way for so long and I had nothing but heartache and prison time to show for my efforts. I hit my knees and I begged God to come into my life. I asked Him to be a real part of my life and guess what…

God kicked the door in! I heard the crash and I looked up and saw no guns, but the biggest light ever witnessed by man. Chief God, Detective Jesus and the Holy Spirit Task Force came into my house, searched and seized my heart and gave me a new conviction–one that carries LIFE. My life changed for the better. God began to restore, repair and revive the relationships I had broken and abused. He allowed me to see how much easier things are if I allow Him to take control.

God has kicked open many doors for me. He will do the same for you. When you feel doors are locked to you and there are no opportunities. When you believe there are things you cannot do. I am a witness; God will kick in some doors for you to walk out of and to walk in through.

Bag and Baggage

The thing that is really hard, and really amazing, is giving up on being perfect and beginning the work of becoming yourself.
—Anna Quindlen

Bag and Baggage! It was a term used in the army to refer to the army's property. It also meant to withdraw honorably with all of your impediments. In prison, it is a term men and woman pray fervently to hear called after their name. Bag and Baggage indicates an inmate is leaving. It means pack your bags with what you are taking and leave what you are not.

Imagine being in prison for over three years. You can accumulate a lot of special things in that amount of time. There are clothes, boots and sneakers, hair clippers, radios, headphones, watches; some may even be fortunate enough to have a TV. There are books and photo albums, school-made cards from children and letters from a grand mother who recently passed away. All of that in three years. What about the person who has been inside a prison for ten years or twenty?

I will tell you from experience, when freedom is in your grasp you don't want a lot of bags holding you down. For me, there came a time when I could care less about sneakers and clothes or radios and watches. No, you could have sent me out the door in a pair of polka-dot boxer shorts and shower slippers and I would have smiled at a blizzard waiting for me outside.

I am being facetious, because in reality there are a few things you will *need* to take with you and some things you should *want* to take with you. Deciphering what those things are is what demonstrates your growth and becomes a deciding factor in whether or not you are leaving your prison for good.

We all have some baggage. Our personal prisons are packed with stuff we hold on to as a way to feel grounded to the familiar. We have a trunk under our bunk with all the anger and resentment we have carried since our first disappointment with life. We have a locker overflowing with bitterness and denial. A tiny shelf holds guilt and humiliation like 'Five and Dime' knick-knacks.

Some of the things were given to us. There is a storage box containing the poor parenting and poverty from our childhood and there is a suitcase stuffed with the abuse from a parent or ex.

Look around you! Are these things still weighing you down? Are you carrying bags filled with low self-esteem, hurt and pain? Are your pockets filled with the scars of your past injuries?

Bag and Baggage! Yes, You! It is time for you to leave your prison; what are you going to take with you? Here is where you recognize your power. You get to decide what you take with you from here on out. All of those things mentioned above can go with you. You can pack 2, 3, 4 duffle bags and take all the bitterness, hurt, anger, depression, guilt, hatred, everything that has prevented you from becoming what God and your destiny has called you to be; you can take it with you.

But believe me, you will only leave for a transfer. It will not be the freedom you desire and deserve. No, you will simply relocate; your same prison with all of its trappings travelling with you.

I know how hard it is to let go. These feelings and experiences have given us the excuse to give up. These emotions hamper our relationships and keep us locked in an unproductive life. We accept the heavy load as part of who we are. Granted, the baggage we carry is a part of who we are, but if the goal is to change then we must leave what we do not need.

Notice I didn't say leave everything. We need to take some things with us. Some of those past hurts have helped us develop tools that will aid us on our journey. We take the strength that came from the abuse and we take the wisdom that evolved from the failures and the resilience that has washed off the shame.

As you leave your personal prison, I want you to envision your bag. It can be a suitcase, briefcase, leather satchel, tote, toolbox, hip-hop backpack, anything you believe fits for you. The only requirement is that it be small. It should be light. You will be able to fit whatever you want into it, but it will never feel heavy.

Open it up and put in the things you want to take with you. Place in your bag the positive skills and tools you have gained by simply living through all of that mess. As I write this, I am looking at the pencil sketch of my bag I drew a few years ago. In it, I placed determination, confidence, responsibility, leadership, assertiveness, empathy, and love. I also drew a small cross on the top to remember that I was taking Jesus with me.

My burdens are light because my bag is light. You can leave all of the negative stuff right there in the hell you are leaving. You might as well; it was the devil's stuff in the first place. Give it back to him.

Chained to the Gang

Yo, my brother was a gang banger and all my homeboys bang I don't know why I do it man, I just do it.
—'Colors' by Ice - T

There is no father at home. Mom has to work two shifts or even worse doesn't work at all. The school system is meager at best. The neighborhood is a housing projects or a square block where the abandoned houses outnumber those that hold residents. There is one playground, the basketball rims are bent and the dirt patches posing as grass are littered with used needles, glassine baggies, empty beer cans and broken bottles. The smell of urine is nauseating. When the sun sets, there is the sound of people arguing, gunshots ring out constantly and police sirens provide a soundtrack for the night.

What type of self-esteem is developed in such deplorable conditions? Who do the children in this arena have to emanate? There is a void in the life of any boy or girl who has to come of age in this environment. These are the conditions; the reasons why gang recruiting is so successful.

The gangs are organized. They have unity and a bond that appears unbreakable. The gangs provide an outlet. They allow that boy or girl to be a part of something bigger than them. The gang offers a sense of security and belonging. Someone is paying attention to that young person so it doesn't matter they are now required to participate in illegal activities; the gain of brotherhood/sisterhood is worth the risk.

The gang brings benefits. There is money, food, parties and most of all prestige. A reputation is the heartbeat of their new life and they are willing to do anything to maintain their standing. They believe their survival depends on it.

The bond that binds the gangs is predicated on loyalty not love. Most of them have never experienced love and have no idea what love is. They don't love themselves and they definitely don't have love for anyone else. Love, to them, is like a type of food only certain people in certain places eat. Those who know about love believe it is foolish to love something when it will only be a matter of time before they lose it. They are not only prepared for loss, they anticipate and expect loss.

A 13-year-old witnesses his or her best friend murdered in a drive by shooting. He/she doesn't cry. It isn't the first time they have lost someone close to them and more than likely won't be the last. Their inability to conjure up a few sympathetic tears or express sadness for their loss is due to the value they have placed on life.

They don't value life! He or she has no respect for life. They will kill you without a second thought. Why? Because they are filled with hate. For themselves and everyone else.

They pick up guns and use them without hesitation. They will have shoot-outs in front of schools or in a crowded mall. You have boys and girls 'busting' their gun as if they are in a video game. No remorse, just a sigh of relief as they prepare to play the next round. The guns give them power, so much so, they refuse to throw the gun down when running from the police. They are caught with the pistol still in their possession and face federal time because they didn't want to be with out that precious 'steel.' They believe their survival depends on it.

I paint a bleak picture. The worst part of my description is that it barely scratches the surface of how crazy this lifestyle truly is. But there is hope, for as long is there is a God to serve, there is hope. Everything I have described is based on learned behavior. Our children are not born with hatred in their blood and an appetite to murder. We must get a hold of them before the gangs do. We have to show them the value and potential of life. We have to grab hold of our children before they become chained to the gangs. We must also be courageous enough to help those who want to break free of that chain before it is too late.

There are many variants of gangs and gang life. From your hard-core original Bloods, Crips, Vice Lords, Gangster Disciples and MS-13's to your neighborhood crews who represent the streets they live on. A person lives on 17th street in the Fifth Ward of the Hillside and hangs out with a bunch of guys/girls who live on 17th street as well. They may call themselves the

1-7 Hill Side Boys or The Fifth Ward Bruhs or the police may name them something similar. They hang out and dress alike, flirt with girls/boys, and fight at school dances with people from the Southside or Uptown. They aren't selling drugs or robbing people (yet), but in the eyes of society they are a gang.

Parents, pay attention to the 'signs.' If your child is talking, dressing, or behaving differently; if he/she is drawing unusual pictures or graffiti, skipping school, hanging out with people you don't know; if your child is suddenly being disrespectful, you need to sit down and seriously talk to your child before it is too late. You have to make sure you give your child the love and attention they crave, because if you don't, there are gangs out there who will.

The gangs love to use children. They train them to carry the guns and drugs and hurt or murder people. If the child is caught and convicted, they face minimal legal repercussions due to their age. He/she will face some juvenile time–a few months or years–then come home to some money and a higher ranking in their gang.

Parents, teachers, mentors, and coaches you better grab that child and hold him or her tight. Show them while they are young the dangers of the gang lifestyle. Show them videos of the 'jump ins', the hospital scenes after a gang banger is shot, the bullet wounds, the blood, the wheel chair and colostomy bag of the drive-by survivors. Show them the young dead bodies if you have to. Show it to them while they are young enough to understand and still be frightened.

Some of you will read this and feel blessed because you live in an area without gangs. Okay. Wonderful, as long as you never plan to travel. The gang problem is no longer isolated to pockets of this nation; gangs are now evident in the seams of our culture.

Some of you may believe you have a handle on your 'gang problem' because you are dealing with the small-town, gang wannabes. Let me tell you, there is no gang culture without violence, thus there is no such thing as a gang wannabe. Once a young person begins emulating the life of a 'gang banger,' even your middle-class suburbanite becomes dangerous.

So Much Self Esteem

**Always turn a negative situation
into a positive situation.
—Michael Jordan**

As it is with most of the ills that plague our society today, we must change our thinking when it comes to the gang problem in America. We must also change our approach; or in many cases develop an approach rather than continue to turn a blind eye. Let me take a minute to converse with you young and old gang members.

First, I commend you for even reading this book. Our current connection may be because you are ready to make some changes in your life and you have volunteered to hear me out in regards to what my insight may be. Or you are in a position where someone has forced you to read this book and that can only mean you are not doing a good job of managing your own life and you are now in a situation where others get to tell you what to do and when to do it. Whatever the reason may be, the book is in your hands and the opportunity to grow is in front of you right now.

Understand you are a survivor. You have witnessed things in your life most people could never imagine, let alone, survive in tact. You have witnessed horrors similar to what soldiers see in the theatre of combat. You have Post-Traumatic Stress that has never been identified nor addressed. You have become cold to certain things, but that coldness can transform into strength, resilience and compassion.

You have learned how to overcome your pain, but you allowed anger to become your motivator. It is time for you to go beneath the anger and deal with the real source of your pain. It is time for you to address the hurt that caused the pain. It is time to look into your mirror and then into your baggage. Take out whatever is blocking your freedom, acknowledge it, apologize, forgive and let it go. Everything you have been through is a part of who you are today. It is time for you to change how you think. Time to let go of the hate that has fueled you for so long and give love a try.

Do you understand that you are still here for a reason? Even if you don't love yourself, can you not see the love God has for you to allow you to still be here at this very moment? Your survival is part of your testimony and it is proof that God has work for you to do. That alone should boost your self-esteem. If not, allow me to add this to it. And this isn't only for the gang members but for everyone who has made mistakes in their lives. Ready? You are not perfect. You were never meant to be perfect. Jesus died so we would not have to be perfect.

What you should be is confident. Confident in your ability to become a better person. You have overcome so much and you deserve to be recognized as a valuable asset to this world. You have to go back to that mirror and look at your worth. You are worthy. Worthy of being loved. Worthy of being respected.

Worthy of being appreciated. Worthy of being welcomed into the Pro Social section of society.

It is time for you to set some new goals. You were a liar; well you now strive to be honest. You were a thief, now you strive to give. You were an alcoholic and drug addict, now you strive to be an example of healthy rehabilitation. You were a gang member now you switch that undying loyalty to a positive family.

Even those of you who have done nothing wrong and are victims. You have to find a reason to get up and face the new day. You must confront the who or what that hurt you and then forgive. You have to take your power back. You may not have asked for what happened to you and it isn't fair, but do you keep it or let it go? If it is not yours, let it go.

You have the ability and the obligation to set a new example. You also have the confidence and self esteem to set goals to help you become that new example. All it takes is some new thinking.

I Think Therefore I am...

If you don't like something, change it; if you can't change it, change the way you think about it.
—Mary Engelbreit

"I wasn't thinking," is the lamest excuse ever created; and it is often accepted. Be clear on this fact, we are always thinking. Even in our sleep, the brain continues to work. The question isn't whether we were thinking; the question is whether our thoughts were positive, rational and free of error. Your ability to escape your personal prison is going to depend on how you think.

We already established a method for disputing our negative thoughts and bad beliefs. We know we can use the ABC's to go in and change how we think, so that we can change our consequences and how we feel. I want you to take it a step further in order to identify the many thinking errors we deal with on a daily basis. **Let's go back into treatment!**

Thinking Errors are the little hurdles of change. Once you can see them, it becomes much easier to jump over them rather than get tripped up repeatedly and continue to fall on your face. I call these thinking errors Irrational Thought Processes or ITP's for short. Allow me to provide you with the technical ITP terms, and then break them down to the everyday/everybody understanding.

The most common ITP is **Awfulizing**. This is the 'stinking thinking' that only negative things can and will happen. Awful is in the name because it is in the thought process. Everything is awful. Think of the person who makes mountains out of anthills and sees everything as being bad. When they come into a room, they bring a gray cloud and bad energy. They say things like, "That will never happen." "I'm going to die if I don't get a raise at my job." "There's no way we can win." "I will make a fool of myself." "You're going to hurt yourself."

If you think like that, you need to get a grip. The sky is not falling everyday on everybody. Do you notice how people stop laughing and enjoying themselves when you come into the room? No one wants to share their good news with you because they know you will try to find a way to rain on their parade. If you suffer from the Awfulizing ITP, you will not have many true friends. The friends you do have, either hold an unconditional love for you or they are miserable too and love your miserable company.

48

"Everyone will be required to read their book report out loud to the class."

(**Awfulizer**) I am going to get up there and sound like a fool. Everyone is going to laugh at me."

"Oh my God, Oh my God! He asked me to marry him!"

(**Awfulizer**) So what. He's going to cheat on you like they all do."

This error in thinking is a set up for failure. The person stays focused on the negative aspects of everything and therefore anticipates depressing consequences. If Awfulizing is your ITP, you must take the time to change your thinking.

You have to stop believing the problem is greater than what it is and you have to look for the advantages and benefits of the situation. Stop acting like you are going to die every time you experience an unpleasant emotion. You must believe in yourself and excel beyond your potential. You may not win every time, but you will definitely have assurance for the next battle. The alternative is to live the life of one who fails because he didn't try. And you will die lonely and alone. How **awful** would that be?

Another troubling ITP is '**Should**.' The thinking error Should is the belief that the world and others should be a certain way. This ITP is usually due to a person's desire for immediate gratification and it is often followed by anger.

If you struggle with this type of thinking error, you will find yourself having thoughts like:

"He/She should have my dinner ready when I get home from work."

"My boss should give me a raise."

"He/she should know how I feel"

That last one is very common and so precarious. Think of the times you have become angry with someone and that person went about their business as if nothing was wrong. Here you are, with steam coming out your ears and this person is singing along with the radio or enjoying something on TV. This person has no idea you are upset, but your thoughts say they should know you are disgruntled and they should know why.

Can you relate? Have you ever moped around with your lip poked out long enough for someone to ask you what's wrong. You believed they should have known what's wrong and so you reacted with evident anger. Then you told the person they should have known this or did that. If the person is me, I'm going to say, "You *should* have told me."

The 'Should' ITP stems from a narcissistic attitude. If you struggle with the 'Should' error, it is time to jump down from your pedestal and play with the rest of the kids in this giant sandbox we call earth. You are a vain person if you believe everyone should think and feel exactly how you think and feel.

We discussed how the *same* conditions could cause different cognitions. It goes without saying, that *different* conditions can cause different cognitions.

For example, say I was raised in a home where we put our dishes in the sink when we were done eating and somebody would wash them later, you were raised differently and believe I should wash out my dish as soon as I'm done. You don't tell me that, but in your Irrational Thought Process you believe I **should** know to wash my dish out right away and I **should** just do it.

Now watch this. If you take the time to dispute that thought and say, "He doesn't know that is what I expect. I will tell him and see if he is willing to do it the way I am used to." Most partners will make that compromise. Okay, maybe only 6 out of 10 if we are referring to men. But speaking for myself, sugar will get you further than '**should**' every time.

Another ITP is the **'Can't'** mentality. This one is somewhat self-explanatory so I won't go too deep. The 'Can't' ITP is when a person makes excuses for why they can't do something; why they can't change. It is also a way to avoid doing something they feel is difficult.

"I can't get an A in World Geography. Even when I study it's too hard."

"I want to quit smoking, but I can't because everywhere I go, people are smoking."

"I can't stop drinking. It's in my blood. My father was an alcoholic and his father was an alcoholic."

We could write another book on the 'Can't' ITP alone. 'Can't' fits right into the 'stinking thinking' category. When you have this type of negative mindset, you again set yourself up for failure. You suppress your potential to be great. You also become stuck. That is how dangerous the 'Can't' ITP is. You forfeit opportunity after opportunity to become better, simply because you believe you can't.

There are many different errors in thinking. When we make mistakes, we must get past trying to deny we were thinking at all and learn to identify the error(s) of our thinking. I have elaborated on a few, but there are many more. There are:

Loaded Words–Name-calling, degrading, using put downs and disregarding another's feelings.

"Screw you, stupid! You don't know what you're talking about."

Absolutes–Thinking in the extreme. Using words like always, never, and everyone.

"I always get away with it. I'll never change."

Blaming–Not accepting responsibility for your actions. Playing the victim.

"If my mom would have showed me more attention I wouldn't be in this mess."

Rhetorical Questions–Expressing your thoughts with questions you really don't want an answer to.

"Who do you think you are talking to like that?"

Then there are the thinking errors that lead to criminality. These are the 'gangster' adaptations of Irrational Thought Processes. These are the criminal thinking errors we lock on to and they in turn keep us locked in to our personal prisons. They are:

Mollification–To justify or rationalize your illegal actions by focusing on external circumstances and the unfairness of society; minimizing the humanity of your victim.

"If I could get a decent job I wouldn't have to sell drugs."

"He has too much money to count. He won't miss this little bit I'm taking."

I plead guilty. I used Mollification throughout my adolescent years and for most of my adult life. I used my poverty to justify my criminality and often looked at my victims as marks or fiends who deserved to be treated as less than human.

Cutoff–A word, phrase or visual image used to eliminate the fear, concern, tension and anxiety to do something criminal or crazy. Usually comes with anger.

"F@#$ it! Let's do it!" "I don't care!"
"Life as a Shorty shouldn't be so rough."

I plead guilty. I used Cut Offs in dealing with my criminal activities as well as my relationships. "I don't care!" was my way of trying to convince myself not to care. And I used song lyrics to hype me up as well. Even today, I struggle with the Cut Off, "Whatever," when I don't want to deal with doing the right thing or hearing sound advice.

Entitlement–The belief that someone owes you. To have a 'God Complex' and think you are above the law. A sense of uniqueness. Confusing your wants with your needs.

"Everybody else is getting paid. I'm gonna get mine."
"After what I've been through, I deserve to get high."

Guilty again. I definitely felt entitled to my way of thinking and lifestyle choice. I believed I was dealt a bad hand and therefore, I had the right to demand the opportunity to 'deal' the cards my way. I convinced myself I really needed something I did whatever it took to get it.

Power Orientation–To use force and aggression over others to get your way. The belief of strong versus weak. Manipulating, intimidating and assaulting others (Power Thrust) in an effort to be in control.

"You're going to do what I say or else."

53

"I make them do all of the work. I just sit back and count money."

I have to plead guilty to this one too. Actually, this was probably my greatest criminal thinking error. The Power Orientation stems from how helpless I felt when I wasn't in control. I convinced myself that not being in control of every situation meant being a victim. It takes strong self-esteem to let go of Power Orientation.

Sentimentality–The desire to offset the negative criminal acts with little good deeds so you can be viewed as a good person. You try to take the focus off the wrongdoing by shifting focus to what you feel is a positive side.

"I am only doing this so my kids will have a better life than I had."

"I brought new uniforms for the entire basketball team. I'm giving back to the hood."

Guilty as charged. I was good for playing the good guy. I had a corner store where I accepted food stamps for cigarettes and extended credit. I gave money to kids and took groups of kids with my own to Chuck E. Cheese and amusement parks. Some of my actions were sincere, but most were self-centered with the ulterior motive of keeping the community on my side and willing to look the other way when I was doing my dirt.

Super Optimism–The unrealistic appraisal of your chances to get away with something. It is an overconfidence that leads you to believe you are invulnerable and unbeatable.

"They will never catch me. I'm too good."

"I can do this for just a little bit longer."

Go ahead and guess… Of course, I plead guilty to this one too. Remember, I was arrested three times for the same offense;

there is no doubt about my Super Optimism. I always tricked myself into believing that since I had gotten away with more than what I had been caught for, that I was still on the winners' side. Those nine years in prison showed me differently. The **S** on my chest doesn't stand for Superman or Super optimistic, it stands for **SANE**.

Cognitive Indolence–Mental laziness. This is your lazy thinking error. It is the desire to take the easy way out. You look for shortcuts in order to avoid having to make any responsible decisions.

"I'll just park the car in this handicap spot."
"Maybe I'll do it if I feel like it."

Guilty. The criminal lifestyle breeds laziness. But it's sort of a covert indolence. I was so used to having things my way I got to a point where I didn't want to weigh the pros and cons of certain decisions. I would just do it. Not out of some courageous act, but because I didn't want to try to come up with a better alternative.

Discontinuity–When you lack focus. You 'discontinue' following through on your goals because you are easily distracted. You become susceptible to the mood of the environment.

"I was going to quit smoking, but I forgot.
"It was Super Bowl weekend and I was doing me like everyone else."

I won't even write it down. You already know. I can't tell you how many times I said I was going to do 'this' to better my life or 'that' to help my children; only to get sidetracked by the criminal lifestyle I was living. The sad part is I believed I was focused. The only thing I was consistent about was not finishing what I had started.

These eight Criminal Thinking Errors are well known and extensively written about. I draw your attention to them only so those of you, who struggle with them, know you are not alone in your sickness and there is a definition for the foolishness you have devoted yourself to for so long. I encourage you to go deeper, to get in that mirror again and take some self-inventory. It is time for some new thinking.

For those of you who have friends and family members who practice these vicious criminal thought patterns, I encourage you to call them on their behavior. Let them know that you know why they act the way they do, that you now see the errors of their ways (thoughts). Then help them to see the errors too.

You don't become SANE without changing how you think. So, as you become more aware of how important it is to take stock of your thoughts, ask yourself these three questions whenever you have doubts as to whether or not your thinking is rational.

1. Are my thoughts based on fact and objective reality?
2. Are my thoughts keeping me out of conflict and protecting my life and health?
3. Are my thoughts helping me achieve my goals and feel the way I want to feel?

The answer must be yes, every time, to all three questions for your thinking to be based on reason. You must train your mind in the same manner you train your body. Treat the thinking errors like unwanted weight and 'work them out/off.' Your personal prison will hold you as long as you desire to stay. It is time for you to demand your release. Change your thinking and be free.

<u>SANE Challenge</u>

1. Write a letter to yourself before you are released from your personal prison. Remind yourself of all the stupid acts you committed and witnessed while in your prison. Then list every reason why you will never go back. Pull your letter out whenever you need to.

2. This next one is for those of you who are ready to confront the gang problem in this country. I challenge you to start with the children. Find a way to bring the children of gang members together at the earliest ages possible. Have citywide talent shows and community festivals; basketball tournaments and girl power sleepovers. I assure you, if we can get the junior generation to establish love bonds based on real connections, they will end the wars their parents began.

I see these modern day gang bangers with MySpace profiles and they have pictures with their signs and flags up, but they also have pictures with their children. They are not as heartless as they want to be and if their children happen to be best friends with the children of their rivals, I see a day where peace becomes the new cool and out of the mouths of babes will come the wisdom and the example for the world to follow.

PART 3

MIS-SED EDUCATION

By learning you will teach;
by teaching you will understand.
—Latin Proverb

Allow me to give an overdue apple to the teachers. I want to tell you how much I love you for what you do. You are the most underappreciated workers in this country. Your influence and impact on our children is second only to 'involved' parents.

It is obvious you did not become teachers for the money. You teach because you love children and you have a passion for educating and contributing to the future. But the job you love has become difficult and trying at times. Some of you have been teaching for decades and it depresses you to see how far the educational system has fallen. Not to mention, the heartbreaking lack of respect from our children today.

Our schools now have metal detectors, police officers and on-site probation officers. The atmosphere gives testimony to the fact that our young people are becoming criminals instead of graduates. You earn less money than those who arrest our children, prosecute our children, judge and sentence our children and those who watch over them when they are incarcerated. Imagine if we provided more money for you, who are tasked with giving our children the tools to prevent them from becoming a part of the justice system that now occupies the very buildings designated for their learning.

Some of you are understandably afraid of the young people whose minds you have been commissioned to mold. Yet, you continue to come back. You continue to chase that feeling of accomplishment that comes from watching a young person's face light up after finally grasping the borrowing method for subtracting fractions.

I share this with you as motivation because you may never hear it from one of your own students. I was fortunate to learn from some wonderful teachers who probably have no idea the influence they had on my life. My sixth-grade teacher who read aloud in a way that was so exciting and eloquent. When she read to us, every word had a life of its own. She also held a fashion show at the school and put me in my first tuxedo, which was a big boost for my struggling, sixth-grade self esteem.

My seventh grade teacher gave our class the most challenging vocabulary words. I'm talking about words many adults would have trouble spelling and providing a definition for. I still remember most of them today. Apathy. Benevolence. Novice. Ambivalent. Prestidigitation. This teacher helped expand my love for words and I still use those same words for my children and students today.

I had an eighth-grade English teacher who demanded your best. She was a 'Grammar Gangster' and she didn't play any games. I still have flashbacks of red ink staining what I believed to be a masterful essay. Although she was hard on us, she had a heart of gold and truly cared about her students. I had the pleasure of seeing her at my oldest daughter's graduation and the students still addressed her with a love that was evident in the way they called her name.

My high school theatre teacher introduced me to two of my first loves–theatre and poetry. On the mornings I made it to school I had the privilege to enter a world of soft music, breathing exercises and passionate (often times hilarious) improvisations. She cast me as Langston Hughes in the school play and I still remember most of the movements she directed us in while reciting 'A Dream Deferred.'

This woman saw something in me and sparked a confidence within me that invited me to dream of becoming more than what the streets had planned for me. Unfortunately, my numerous absences led to my expulsion from the arts program before having the opportunity to perform the play. It would be years before I would see her again, but I never forgot the day she looked me in my eyes and said, "Jonathan, you are a gifted and talented young man and you can do great things."

While I was in prison, I taught GED, Creative Writing and Intro to Theatre. I used an eloquent reading style and stressed an extensive vocabulary. I was notorious for my demand of proper sentence structure and my ever-present red ink pen. And, although I stressed the Stanislavski acting method, most of my warm-up exercises and improvs were borrowed from a beautiful teacher and a small studio classroom in Uptown Harrisburg, Pennsylvania.

I say all of that to say thank you, and please do not be discouraged or believe your labor is in vain. There are students like myself, who have left your classes prematurely and you may never see them again. However, if you did your job, they too will one day have to look in the mirror of their lives and confess that someone believed in them enough to try to teach them the power of education. You are mind shapers and therefore world changers. I, for one, will always applaud the work you do with our children. Our futures remain in your hands.

What Do You Want To Be

Education is the passport to the future, for tomorrow belongs to those who prepare for it today.
—Malcom X

I want you to take a few minutes and reflect back on your childhood. Try to remember what you said when your parents or a teacher asked you; 'what do you want to be when you grow up?' For the teens and young adults reading this book, apply the question to yourself today. What do you want to be when you grow up?

As a child, I had multiple answers to that question. I wanted to be a lawyer, a detective, an astronaut, a famous rapper, a teacher and a scientist. When I was really feeling special, I would proudly proclaim that I was going to become the first black President of the United States of America.

As children, we have such a powerful faith and we believe that anything is possible. It is a confidence unscathed by failure or disappointment and it is an attitude that I encourage young people as well as the older generations to hold fast to.

I spoke to a group of teens recently and I raised the 'what do you want to be' question. They gave me answers like clinical psychiatrist, forensic anthropologist, software developer; one 13-year-old girl proclaimed she was going to be a successful businesswoman slash philanthropist like Oprah. I expected to hear the common doctor, lawyer, firefighter answers. I was very impressed.

I brought it to their attention that none of them said they wanted to be a criminal, a drug addict or a high school drop out. Yet, the statistics in that particular school, and many like it, reflect that many of them would drop out and eventually get involved with alcohol, drugs, crime or a combination of the three. They all shook their heads and said "not me." At that age, I would have shaken my head as well. Unfortunately, the numbers do not lie and unless we set a new example one out of every three of those kids will fail; not only in school but also in life.

Dire Education

He was the most popular guy at a school he no longer attended. He dropped out in the eleventh grade because, in his words, "the streets were calling." At the age of 17, he became one of the biggest drug dealers in his city. During what would have been his senior year, he often drove up to the school in his Jaguar XJ8 or his 745i BMW and took his friends to McDonalds or the pizza place for lunch.

He showed up at all the football and basketball games looking like a hip-hop superstar. He wore diamond earrings and Platinum chains; 300-dollar-shoes, 200-dollar-jeans and shirts. He wore mink coats and leather jackets that cost thousands of dollars. He had three or four girlfriends who all looked like models or women plucked straight from a music video.

He attended, what should have been *his* graduation, to show support for his childhood homies who were receiving their diplomas and to scope out all of the pretty women who would be there. I will let him tell the rest in his own words.

"I felt real crazy. I stood there looking at all of the dudes I called L 7's (squares) and they were so happy. It was the biggest graduating class the school had ever had. I stood there in an Armani suit listening to the mayor give a powerful speech about overcoming adversity and proving the world wrong. He bragged about them destroying the myth that young urbanites could never amount to anything. He told them they were equipped to now face the world at eye level not from a kneeling position. That part stood out to me, because even though I was standing tall, I felt a daily pressure on me that had my soul on its knees.

The graduates walked across the stage, some of them did pre-planned dances and I couldn't help but smile even though I was sick on the inside. Most of the guys went out of their way to shake my hand as I stood at the gate. They yelled at parents and siblings to take a picture of us together like I was a celebrity. I smiled and teased them, but all I could think about was how much I wanted to be one of them. I wanted to wear a cap and gown and a big Kool-Aid smile with my parents crying and hugging me. Instead, I walked out of there a loser pretending to be a winner. A few months later I walked into a 15-year-prison sentence."

One of my disinclined GED students told this story to me. He thought that because I was teaching the class I was some college-educated, white-collar criminal. Imagine his surprise when I shared with him that I, too, had dropped out of school for 'street dreams' unfulfilled.

I was 16 years old and repeating the tenth grade. I convinced myself I was too far behind and there was no way for me to catch up. After a heated argument, my mother reluctantly agreed to sign me out. I returned my books and took my last stroll through the revered halls of John Harris High School as a dropout.

I dropped out of high school because I was ashamed and embarrassed. Plain and simple. I didn't want my classmates to see me going to sophomore classes while they were juniors. The sad thing is I wasn't embarrassed about being a teen-age father. I wasn't ashamed that I could be found standing on corners in front of bars offering to pay someone to go in and buy me beer. I wasn't ashamed of being a drug dealer.

I went from believing and striving to become a lawyer, a hip-hop star or the first African-American President to being a high school dropout, a teen-age father, an alcoholic, an addict and eventually a career criminal. I gave up on my dreams and chose to buy into the negative aspirations that were, in my opinion, so much easier to accomplish. I looked at my surroundings and thought to myself, 'these people don't care. Why should I?'

Why Dropping Out Often Leads to Going In

My people are destroyed for lack of knowledge:
because thou hast rejected knowledge...
—Hosea 4:6

I became part of an ugly statistic—the drop out rate. Particularly high amongst Black and Hispanic male students, the drop out rate continues to be a crisis in this nation. In many schools, only two out of three will graduate with their class. One third of our young minds are quitting school. What is even worse is that in many cities a third would be a wonderful number. There are schools that have over a fifty percent dropout rate. I am talking about high schools that are labeled 'drop-out factories' and graduation is a 50-50 chance. That is not sane! Why are our children leaving school?

Poverty is definitely one of the main reasons. When there is a low socio-economic status, there is a greater risk of failure for promising literacy achievement. Translation–Growing up in the 'hood can lead to the lack of an education. The 'hood is where poverty is like a plague and single parent homes are the norm. Even when there are two parents in the house, their educational and occupational status may limit their resources, or knowledge thereof, to provide the necessary arrangements for the child to succeed in school.

They are limited in time and understanding to read to their child or make sure he/she is prepared for class in the morning. The poverty also leads to a poor diet. There are kids who go to school after eating a bag of chips for breakfast. Some of them don't eat anything. They go to school hungry. They're light headed and unfocused until after lunch. For a growing school aged child, breakfast is the most important part of the day. Mark Twain and math problems are hard to digest when you're hungry.

Eventually, that child… no, let me speak for myself and if it resonates then I'm sure you will relate. I eventually noticed my surroundings. I came to an understanding that my family, my school and my community were not a part of the prosperous and privileged I had read or heard about. I realized I was poor; that my family and my community were poor.

There were very few business owners in my neighborhood, but there were a whole lot of drug dealers. I didn't see many college graduates in my neighborhood but I saw many drug addicts. I saw 15 and 16 year olds driving luxury cars and wearing expensive clothes and sneakers. They had money and pretty girls and they weren't hungry at all. They were eating well.

I chose to join them. I wanted to 'eat well' too and I didn't want to wait. I took the easy route. I became a PIG (Pursuer of Immediate Gratification). I dropped out of school because I believed I could attain immediate success. I wanted the results without doing the work.

I must be honest with you because I know many of you will read this and relate to my choice as being a survival tactic for a situation I had no control over. Make no mistake about it; I made my choice in error. I had other options. Poverty and unequal education did not give me a license to sell drugs. I could have stuck it out. Yes, things may have been difficult for me. I may not have had Air Jordans or Tommy Hilfiger and Polo. I may have had to go to the Food Banks, Food Pantries, Goodwill, and Salvation Army.

If that sounds harsh or embarrassing, well I would trade in my total ten and a half years of prison for a few years of embarrassment. Not to mention, being able to shed the guilt I gained by poisoning my already suffering community.

There are many motivations for deciding to drop out of high school. Having a child also played a part in my decision. I wanted to play house and pretend as if I was going to go work and help raise my child. I know there are a lot of young women who become pregnant while in school and decide to drop out. I also know of high schools that have full nurseries for the women who are courageous enough to stay in school despite being a teen parent.

I have also met a lot of older people who dropped out to go to work, especially those who were on farms down south. Many of you dropped out for less selfish reasons than I did and I want to encourage you to go back. Education is such a vital part of your success and ultimately your survival. It is never too late to further your education. If you still have breath in your body, you can still learn and if you dropped out of high school and are not able to go back, get your GED. Then go on from there if you so desire. It is one thing to be mis-educated and another to miss being educated.

I want my GED

Statistics say over 60 percent of black, male, high school dropouts would spend time in prison before their thirtieth birthday. I taught GED in the prisons and I would say the number is probably higher than 60 percent. Most of the prisons had waiting lists to get into the GED classes.

The federal prison system, as well as many state prisons, requires any person who has not achieved a high school diploma or its equivalent to attend GED classes for a minimum of 280 hours. They may then opt out with the understanding they forfeit any good time earned while they are not attending classes. Basically, you either go to GED until you pass or you stay in prison for your entire sentence.

These men have never balanced a checkbook or learned to calculate the tip percentage of a restaurant bill. We are talking about grown men who read below a third grade level and have never learned simple fractions. Men who couldn't name five past U.S. Presidents if their lives depended on it. Men who write essays with no paragraphs or punctuation. If the essay topic is " Who is Your Role Model and Why" these men will struggle for days just trying to think of someone they would consider a role model and 8 out of 10 of them will choose their mother. The point is, these men are way behind and I believe that in the women institutions the circumstances are very similar.

As a GED Tutor, I had to find ways to engage men who had no desire to be in the classroom, let alone learn something. Some of them were unreachable. They came into the class and read the newspaper or put their heads down and slept. I would see many of these men get released, go home and come back before I had the chance to cross their name off their folder to give to someone else.

I realized how valuable an education is to those of us who already have a strike for being convicted felons. I made it my personal mission to engage them in the learning process and the importance of education.

I taught them algebra by explaining they had been doing equations since second grade and drawing empty boxes instead of x's and y's as the variables. I changed the Order of Operations' PEMDAS acronym to mean; Punish Every Math Dilemma And Succeed instead of Please Excuse My Dear Aunt Sally. I used street drug analogies to teach fractions, units of measure, and percentages. I drew a snowman with a belt to teach circumference (the buckle was the radius) and I taught my students how to draw pictures to help them solve word problems.

We did poetry readings and acted out scenes from the English Reading book. We discussed history as if we were there and could change the outcomes if we studied exactly what happened. I made up essay topics that interested them, i.e. 'Why Are the Cowboys Better Than the Redskins.' If you stayed on topic, provided three reasons (the Body) in five paragraphs (the Introduction, the Body and the Conclusion) with four sentences in each, you were guaranteed a passing grade.

I was passionate, determined and innovative. Every teacher I worked for was able to sit at their desk and do whatever work they needed to catch up on, because they knew I had control of the class. I designed curriculums, created tracking sheets to determine when a student was ready to test and scheduled the testing for hundreds of students.

Of course, some men weren't trying to hear it. They could care less about a GED and often, I couldn't blame them. Imagine telling a 19-year-old kid, who just received a 30-year prison sentence, to write an essay about his favorite season of the year. I gave them space and patience. I simply asked them not to disrupt the class and I encouraged them to read something while there; a book, newspaper, magazine, and especially some relative case laws.

Many of them noticed the success of the other students. They witnessed men, who started out barely able to read, receive their GED. They saw these men put on a cap and gown then walk the stage in ceremonial fashion in front of their family and friends. Many of them began to believe they could enjoy that same success.

In prison, Fridays were usually a relaxed day for my GED classes. When we didn't watch a movie, I held a weekly spelling bee. I would split the class into two groups and have them compete for note pads and pens. The students were required to spell the word, give the definition, and use the word in a sentence. If they failed to do any of the three, the opposing team would have the chance to steal those points.

Let me share with you one of the breakthrough moments I had with a student during one of those weekly spelling bees. Let's call him Tee. He was one of my indifferent students. He would come into the classroom crack some jokes with his friends before we began then sit there and either read a Hip-hop magazine or stare out of the window. We had been studying geography that week so I was using countries as the theme for the spelling bee.

They were having a good time trying to sound out Madagascar and Czechoslovakia. I would give the stronger students the more difficult words and the slower learners the less difficult countries. The word was Peru and the student I had given it to was arguing whether or not there was such a place. He didn't know how to spell it and his team was already down a few points.

Tee had been following along, but no matter how many times we invited him, he still refused to participate. When I allowed the other team to steal the points for spelling Peru and then earn two more points for telling me what continent Peru is located on, Tee shook his head as if to say something wasn't fair. He was sitting on the side of the team that was losing and I offered him the opportunity to help the team out.

He stared at me as if he believed I was running game, but he decided to play along. "What's the word, Tutor?"

I thought about it and since I had no idea what level he was on, I decided to play it safe and gave him what I considered an easy one. "Your country is Iran."

The class let out a burst of excitement. Both teams agreed the word was easy. Tee stared at me with a look that expressed betrayal. I was beginning to think I might have made a mistake. He may not have heard of Iran. A few of the students had said aloud that they never heard of it but it seemed easy to spell. Tee started looking down at his desk and I assumed he might have changed his mind.

One of the other men whispered, "Come on, man. You can spell that." Tee shot him a look that sent chills through *my* body. The boy turned his head and found something interesting on the floor to look at. I usually do the Jeopardy game show music when a lot of time has passed, but I gave him a few more seconds.

Finally, he laughed and said, "That's too easy. Iran, I-R-A-N."

"That is correct." I stated as I drew two slashes on the board. "Please tell me what continent Iran is on or use Iran in a sentence for two more points."

He thought about it for a few seconds, then gave me a sentence, "When the police came to my block, I ran."

The class erupted in raucous laughter. It was a good thing that Tee took it as supporting amusement. I cut them off quickly. I shook my head and reminded Tee that, although his answer was good, he has to remember we are talking about countries.

Tee looked at me and nodded his head. "I know that, Tutor. These clowns didn't let me finish my sentence. I was saying, when the police came to my block I ran… to the country, Iran."

I gave him the points and he eventually received his GED.

I share that story because I am extremely proud of every single person who has achieved his/her GED. The GED is a second chance diploma. I have witnessed many men and women fall in love with learning and pursue a college degree after achieving their GED. They get that taste of higher education and they crave more, which is always a good thing because the alternative is to remain ignorant.

'Not Cool'

Either you're slingin crack rock or you got a wicked jumpshot
—'Things Done Changed' by Notorious B.I.G.

One of the most important changes we must make is destroying the myth that being intelligent is 'Not Cool.' I am a strong proponent of recognizing the importance of the African-American contribution to the English language. There is no denying the positive cultural impact of certain slang and Ebonics, but we must counter the image that speaking proper English is equivalent to being a nerd or wanting to be white.

We must emphasize the importance of having an extensive vocabulary and being able to communicate in arenas outside of our neighborhoods. Your career goals become very limited when your conversation is filled with a lot of, "Yo, What up doe? youknowwhatImean, real talk, you feel me, Son, my nigga," along with a lot of unnecessary profanity.

There should be no embarrassment for being intelligent. I consider myself well read and very intelligent. I pride myself with being able to navigate effectively through the multifaceted areas of my life. I consider myself cool.

I can sit in a boardroom with my colleagues and discuss profit margins, scrap percentages, quick and current ratios. I can then teach some of those same concepts to my GED class by breaking the explanation down into pizzas, the delivery person and their tips. I can leave work, go hang out with some of my homies and even with a suit and tie on, feel just as at ease as when we were 9 and 10 years old playing in the dirty puddles of the Dry Cleaner's parking lot.

I can later help my children with their homework without having to look up their third grade spelling words or google the Pythagorean Theorem.

I can talk stimulus bills and Wall Street principles. I can elaborate on the musical contributions of the Jackson Five and Jay Z; Chubby Checker and Chuck D; The Beatles and Run DMC; Diana Ross to Rick Ross, Little Richard to Lil' Wayne, and John Lennon to John Legend. Speaking of music, I can still hold my own on a mic in a studio as well as give the Morning Prayer at church.

Is there anything wrong with that? We must accept the fact that we live in a time where versatility is needed and expected. Ignorance is the second cousin of 'crazy.' It is time to readjust your mindset. Time to realize that being an intelligent, well-spoken person who recognizes the world is much larger than the block you grew up on and you should therefore make every effort to diversify your communication proficiency in order to be most effectual in all areas of your life. Now, be honest, that previous sentence was so not ignorant. I believe it sounded somewhat cool. youknowwhatImean!

Of course, the ignorance badge doesn't end with our notions of intelligence or proper speaking. There are also the ignorant images we have grown to accept, condone and encourage. I won't bombard you with a plethora of actions and behaviors that would be considered ignorant, but I will mention a few that are definitely 'Not Cool.'

Wearing your pants sagging with your underwear showing is 'Not Cool.' Wearing tight clothes to show off your curves is 'Not Cool.' Thinking you need to show off your curves for boys to like you is 'Not Cool.' Liking a girl only because she has a nice body is 'Not Cool.' Showing disrespect to your elders is so 'Not Cool.' Texting in school and church is 'Not Cool.' Smoking… anything is 'Not Cool.' Drinking and driving is 'Not Cool.' Underage drinking is 'Not Cool' at all. Cursing is 'Not Cool.'

Having sex before you are married is 'Not Cool.' Having sex before you're old enough to be married is 'Not Cool.' Having unprotected sex is 'Not Cool.' Having sex with multiple people is ignorant, dangerous and 'Not Cool.' Dropping out of school is 'Not Cool.' Stealing is 'Not Cool.' Lying is 'Not Cool.' Fighting is 'Not Cool!' Doing drugs is 'Not Cool.' Selling drugs is 'Not Cool.' Going to prison is 'Not Cool!'

I could go on and on, but I'm sure you catch my drift. Setting a new example is all about standing up and standing out. You stand up to the peer pressure and say when something is 'Not Cool' and you stand out by walking away from the crowd that does not agree with you.

I know it is difficult to be bold in your beliefs when it seems everyone else is doing negative things and being worshipped as being cool because of their misdeeds. That is why education is so important. When you apply intellectual reasoning, you know what is right and what is wrong. You also base your choices on long-term goals instead of short-term gains. Don't you dare give in to the crowd! You continue to set a new example and I assure you, in the end, you will be a role model and a success story as well. Now, how cool is that?

Probation Until Graduation

These are a few SANE Suggestions that can be converted into **SANE Challenges**. I believe these ideas could help with the crisis we face within our educational system.

I believe we must improve the quality of education starting at the early childhood level. There must be a stronger math and science curriculum as well as an emphasis on early reading. Today's technology advances require a much higher intelligence and stronger work ethic at earlier stages of childhood development if we want to compete with other nations.

Teachers should have mandatory re-training in their fields to learn new practices and trends as well as sharpen old skills. They should also spend a minimum of one week per year with a younger grade level to establish a relationship with future students. It is easier to maintain the respect of an errant adolescent student who you established a relationship with as a child. We must also show a deeper appreciation of our teachers by rewarding them with a higher rate of pay and more benefits. We have a 'No child Left Behind Act.' We need a 'No Teacher Left Behind Act' to go with it.

We should establish more apprenticeship and Vo-tech programs that give hands-on-training to students starting in their sophomore year of high school. Provide a tax relief to businesses willing to employ students and allow them to pay lower than minimum wage to students who still live at home. Provide Summer Work Programs similar to the successful programs of the 1970's.

We should set up After After-School programs. These will consist of actual school classes in relaxed settings that continue

2-3 hours after the regular school day. It will provide additional time for working parents (especially single parents) and become a continuation of what many consider a short school day. This will also provide employment (maybe some of the aforementioned high school students) and improve the education of our future labor force. Again, we have to create a new attitude that school is 'cool.' So a few extra hours will not only be beneficial for working parents but also to struggling and 'hungry for education' children.

We can call it the 'Seconds Program.' You know how when we eat something and if it is good, we go back for a second helping? Why not adopt that attitude about education and let the kids satisfy that hunger with 'Seconds.'

For those young people who are beginning to go astray we must come up with ways to hold them accountable and teach them the law of choices and consequences. A child skips school and is suspended from the school he wasn't trying to be at in the first place. Then the parent is fined a ridiculous sum of money. That practice falls into the realm of 'crazy' as well.

It is time we impose truancy laws that punish the student rather than the parent. Give the students the fine and then make them work it off. It should be obvious if a child is skipping school his/her parents may have lost their influence over the child. If said child is skipping school, the parent(s) need help and for the parents who do still maintain a level of authority over their child, I'm sure they would agree with allowing their child to be held accountable for his/her actions.

While we are discussing laws and consequences for students' misbehavior, we must find a way to keep our children in school even after they have done something wrong. We should give judges the discretion to sentence juvenile delinquents to finish school in order to avoid jail time. They can establish 'Probation until Graduation' programs. With the more serious infractions have the child be subject to drug testing, anger management/ drug education classes, anti gang initiatives and anything to give the child a preview of what their future will hold if they continue to violate the law.

Most importantly, we must celebrate the educational accomplishments of our students. The science fair should have as large a crowd as the Homecoming basketball game. We must reward our children for doing well. If your child gets good grades or does something great in school, make sure it becomes news even if only to family. Send text messages and emails and encourage your relatives to call and congratulate the child for a job well done. Send letters to the editor of your local newspaper and blog on line about your child's grades or school accomplishments. Have report card parties where admission requires report cards with no grades less than a B or C. Find a way to set a new example that school is cool and excelling in school is awesome!

PART 4

OVERCOMING THE ADDICTION, CONQUERING THE COMPULSION

Your willingness to look at your darkness is what empowers you to change.
—Iyanla Vanzant

Addiction: *(1) a state of physiological or psychological dependence on a potentially harmful drug. (2) devotion: great interest in a particular thing to which a lot of time is devoted.*

Drug and alcohol addiction attack you from two angles. There is the physical aspect, where a dependence is created and a person can become physically sick (cravings, withdrawal) when they don't have the drug. There is also a psychological dependence where a person believes they need the drug to function. They become devoted to the point where they get caught up in depending on a drug to make them feel or operate better, yet that same substance is killing them.

With the addiction comes the compulsion to repeat certain irrational behaviors regardless of the negative consequences. No one makes rational decisions while under the influence of drugs. Actually, most of the choices we make while on drugs are crazy.

The addict has no sense of dignity and pride and loses all inhibitions. He/she no longer values family or pro social living. Drug addicts will lie, steal, cheat, rob and kill to get their fix. They will sell everything they own from their TV to their car to their bodies and even their children.

I can remember many occasions when I put getting drunk and high in front of taking care of home and spending time with my children. If I wasn't out 'clubbing', I was having house parties and get-togethers where alcohol and drugs were always plentiful. Even when I had my children with me and I was pretending to be a good father, I still exposed them to my chaotic lifestyle. I drank and smoked marijuana around them and I made drug transactions while they were with me. I was crazy and it hurts right now to even think about how ignorant and selfish I was.

While in our addictions, we learn to disrespect ourselves. We also suffer from self-hatred. On the streets I was known as Ace. I actually developed another identity. That is how much self-hatred I had. I let Ace be my alter ego, my bad superman. I was under the impression the more money I made and the more women I acquired; the more respected I would be.

Deep down I knew what I was doing was wrong and so I created a false image to avoid facing the disappointment I knew I had become. I turned to the drugs and alcohol to keep from feeling the hurt and shame I carried within.

We drink and use drugs because we want to feel better. Even if we already feel good, we believe that the drugs will make us feel even better. And most of the time the drugs have that effect, but it is a short term gain which leads to a worse feeling and requires more drugs to feel simply normal again.

The typical addict gets involved with drugs because they are curious. The addict becomes hooked because of a void in their life that they try to fill up or forget by numbing themselves with the narcotics.

If you are an addict, you must try to identify the void in your life that is sucking you deeper into the abyss of addiction. You are a high school student taking pills because you have a void in your life. You are a single mother spending almost your entire check on crack cocaine because something is missing in your life. You are a soldier who has done three tours in Iraq and you are hooked on heroin because something is missing in your life.

The drugs do not restore the missing part of your life. They offer a temporary amnesia of what is absent and hurting you because it isn't there. The drugs are tricking you into believing you feel good. When the drug wears off the void is still there. It is time for you to put the pipe down, throw out the 'blunts', break the mirror you sniff cocaine and heroin off and confront the emptiness that has consumed you.

We have to realize we have the power to feel good without drugs or alcohol. That power is in how we think. We change how we think to change how we feel. Sometimes it requires us to think about how our actions affect our loved ones. We must shed off our self-centeredness and realize how much pain we cause the people who love and care about us. Our self-hatred can be conquered by recognizing we love someone else enough to stop hurting them. That is victim impact, and for me it has made a world of difference.

The Impact of Victim Impact

Ace,

Wassup Cousin? I know it's been a minute since I wrote you, but your last letter had me thinking. Of course, I still look up to you. You are my idol. I remember when I was 12 years old and you would pull up to my house in your brand new, white Chrysler New Yorker with the sound system banging and the talking computer lady, "Your door is ajar." That was crazy! I would wait for you to come in so I could see what fly outfit you would have on. Ooh and I loved it when you'd give me money and let me wear your gold necklace while you were in the house.

My mom would be stressing until you got there. I watched her beep you over and over again, leaving 911 as the code. Her and her boyfriend would be arguing about whether they should wait for you or go out on their own. I knew they were getting drugs from you. I would take my little sister in the bedroom so she didn't have to see them like that. I remember times when you were mad when you came over 'cause my mom owed you money and she didn't have it, but still asked for more. You would give it to them on credit because you was a good guy. Every week, they would owe you almost their whole check and when you would come to get your money, I would be mad. Not at you, though. At them because me and my sister needed things but we had to go without.

Remember when I was 13 and I got into a fight with my mom and I ran away from home. You let me come and stay at your super fly bachelor crib. You even argued with my grand mom about me staying with you. You told her that you went through the same thing with your mom and understood what I was going through. You handled it like a soldier. I wanted to be just like you. But you said I couldn't. You said I had to stay in school and never sell drugs. I knew you were just saying that 'cause I was young. You just wanted me to learn how to do it right, first. So, I watched you and I learned from the best.

I remember being at your crib when you had those crazy wild parties. Everyone would be drinking and smoking weed and cracking jokes on each other. I loved it, especially when you would let me have my own beer. I would have everyone laughing at my jokes.

It was at one of those parties when I saw my dad. He had been saying he'd come get me and take me to buy a pair of sneakers, but he never did. When he came over that night, he barely said anything to me. He was there to see you. I remember y'all going to the back and I knew he was buying crack from you, probably with the money he could have used for my sneakers. I didn't care for real, because I knew you would get me some sneakers. But when you started cracking jokes about him and he just laughed, I lost all respect for him.

I really started worshipping you when I saw how easy it was for you to sell drugs to not only my mom and dad but to your mom and dad as well. You explained to me how you used most of their money for your younger brothers and you only sold to them to make sure you kept the money in the family and to keep your mom from having to deal with the savages on the streets. That is when I decided I could do the same thing.

I patterned my whole style of hustling and dealing drugs after you and I still use it to this day. I give credit to build clientele but I'm not a pushover, I set up a crew of hungry young thugs and put them to work, so I rarely have to get my hands dirty. I take care of the hood and the younger family just like you did. I only drink and smoke weed like you did. I know the rule: Never get high on my own supply. I only let people I trust come to my house for business. And check this out, talk about passing the torch; I have your younger brother under my wing like you had me. I got him in training. And of course, I'm taking care of my own kids just like you showed me. I keep them laced in the hottest gear.

I know you heard about me getting pulled over with that 8-ball on me. I did 6 months in the county jail. It was nothing. It just taught me to be more careful. Yo, when I gave the cop my last name, he asked about you. You're notorious, Cuz! But I'm in the system now, so watch out. Nah, I'm joking, I ain't trying to do no more time and I'm too smooth to get caught again.

On the real, I got everything ready for when you come home. We can take over the world if you're with it. I'm here for you and I'm almost on top like you were. I owe all of my success to you! Thanks for being my inspiration, Cuz!

One Love, Lil' Cuz

The assignment was to write a letter to myself from one of my victims. I could have written a letter from my mother. We've had plenty of talks. We've cried, apologized, and made promises to forgive and do better. I have a pretty good idea how much I hurt my mom and writing a letter from her would have taken very little effort.

I could have written a letter from any one of my children. I actually have plenty of real letters from my children, who even in their pre-pubescent years had no problem letting me know how much I had hurt them and let them down. To write a victim letter from one of them would have also been too easy.

Most of us, even in our insanity can acknowledge how much we hurt those who are closest to us. Whether as an addict or criminal, we know certain loved ones are undeniable victims of our trifling choices.

I chose to share this letter written from the point of view of one of my younger cousins because it encompasses many of the negative and criminal thinking patterns that are passed in a perpetual cycle of ignorance. I also chose this letter because of how difficult it was for me to see and admit this person is one of my victims. I was oblivious to how far reaching my actions were. I didn't get it. I was sick, which leads me to a new treatment program that is so needed in so many places.

Drug Dealers Anonymous

Cash Rules Everything Around Me! C.R.E.A.M.
Get the money! Dollar dollar bill, yall!
C.R.E.A.M.–by Wu Tang Clan

"Welcome to Drug Dealers Anonymous. My name is Jonathan Queen and I am a drug dealer."

"Hi Jonathan!"

Drug dealing is a disease! I said it! You can call it controversial if you want, but that is what I believe and how I feel. Selling drugs is a compulsion more serious than the compulsion to gamble. It is a continuous act that will usually require some type of cold turkey break (Prison) or some intense treatment. If there is a Gamblers Anonymous, then there should definitely be a Drug Dealers Anonymous.

I won't bore you with quotes from scientific studies conducted over the past 20 years. I will make it plain. When a person gambles, something happens inside their brain. It is the equivalent of smoking cocaine, eating chocolate and thinking about sex. There are reward and loss nerves that react to the thought of gambling, the thought of risking something in anticipation of receiving a reward. That is considered gambling. It is also a true definition for dealing drugs. The art of dealing drugs is a gamble in its purest form. ***Let's go to the streets!***

I take 100 dollars and purchase an 8-Ball (eighth of an ounce of cocaine). I then bag it up in 15 smaller bags to sell for 20 dollars each. If I sell all of them, I will make 300 dollars. Therefore, if I am successful, this gamble will bring me a 200-dollar profit. And yes it is a gamble, because if I am caught by the police while engaged in this illegal course of action I risk losing my freedom and if I am caught by a stick-up kid or an addict with no money and nothing to lose, I may lose my life. Do you honestly not see how electrifying this process is to the synaptic nerves?

It gets worse. Visualize a poker table with five people gambling and hundreds gathered around observing. Two of the five players fold their hand after the deal. The third player folds after one draw. The last two players call, raise, call, raise until one of them calls 'all in.' They finally show their hands. The 'all in' player wins the pot and literally goes from having nothing to being on top. The loser still has a substantial amount of chips and will be in the game for a while longer. Both players are heroes to the hundreds watching, many of whom have nothing, but now believe they too, can become rich in one hand.

The same high that comes from winning 10 straight hands of black jack is the same power burst that comes from winning a large poker hand with a bluff. The same adrenaline rush that comes from shooting 'craps' and getting down to your last 10 dollars then rolling seven 7's in a row is what a drug dealer feels when he hits the corner with a pocket full of 'stones' and returns home in a few hours with pockets full of cash.

The possibility of a high return and fast success is what captivates the drug dealers. The criminal arena, also referred to as the 'Game', is like a spectator sport where everyone is watching you. Some of them watch because they admire you and aspire to achieve your success; others because they are on an opposing team and are anticipating your downfall. This state of mind only adds to the rush a drug dealer feels. Awed by the glamour mixed with danger, he bets constantly in an effort to acquire more and more. He knows there is a chance he may 'crap out' and that, too, increases the dopamine. That is why, no matter how many times he loses, he will try, try again.

This illness isn't gender specific either. Women are now the fastest growing prison population in America. Ladies, you too need to attend this inaugural DDA Meeting. You too, have become addicted to the lifestyle of fast money and high-risk activities. Some of you become enamored with simply being on the arm of a drug dealer. You like the idea of not having to work but still being able to get your hair and nails done regularly. You enjoy the expensive clothes and shoes, the exclusive meals and exotic vacations. You risk your life, and many times the lives of your family and children, because you want to ride with a 'hustla' or 'balla.'

You're sickness leads you to stand at the craps table and blow on the dice while placing side bets on the outcome of the high roller you came with.

Some of you beautiful, gifted women choose to pick up the dice yourself. You run your own operations. You hit the corners, you supply weight to the streets, and you carry your own gun and won't hesitate to use it. You are on a mission to be a 'Queen-Pin' and your disease is as deep as your male counterparts. Welcome Miss, to Drug Dealers Anonymous. Please pay attention.

I recently spoke at a literary program and after talking about my journey in and out of prison, I started taking questions. A middle-aged woman stood up and said she has a son who is in prison for the third time with a seven-year sentence. She choked up a little as she stated, "We just did 13 years and he wasn't even home for 9 months." The tears began to fall.

"What is it that I'm doing wrong," she cried. "Why does he come home and do so good for a little while and then go right back to doing the same old things."

It is sad, but there is no easy answer to that question. Even sadder is the fact this lady used the word *we* when describing *his* prison sentence. This mentality, which is her reality, is another example of victim impact.

You committed a crime and were consequently, sentenced to a certain amount of time away from society for **your** actions. Yet, your mother, father, wife, children suffer so much, that they too, feel like they are doing time. Because of their love and sometimes, their guilt, they lock into personal prisons with a sentence to mirror your own.

After reminding the woman she was not responsible for the decisions her 'grown' son made, I answered her question from my experience. I told her that because I had spent so much time in the criminal lifestyle, I believed selling drugs was what I knew how to do best. Drug Dealing was my comfort zone. No matter how hard I tried or how much I believed I could do different, positive things; if life became difficult; if I felt like my back was against the wall, I immediately reverted to my Plan A–selling drugs. I may have pretended as if it was a Plan B, but it was always in the forefront of my options.

"If she doesn't get it from me, she's going to go out on the streets and get it from someone else. I am protecting her from being out there with those savages. Besides, I'm keeping the money in the family."

Those were my words as I sold drugs to my mother. To my own mother! Are those not the twisted thoughts of one who is sick? I sold drugs to both my parents. I sold drugs while playing with my children in the park. I allowed addicts and drug dealers to come to my house where my children slept. I kept guns in the house. And after being arrested and spending time in prison. I came home and did it again.

I tell you drug dealing is a sickness and the criminal lifestyle that comes with it is a disease that many men and woman are struggling with. You have men and women, boys and girls who have been selling drugs for years. Drug dealing is how they feed their families and they are committed to their hustle. It isn't easy to tell them to just stop. For many it will take either death or jail to bring them to a halt.

This is why the reeducation process is so important. We have to learn that what we considered the easiest and most comfortable thing to do is really the most difficult, dangerous, and the most heartbreaking to the people who love us and want us to succeed.

I argue with many of my peers who believe we cannot expect a young gang member or drug dealer to walk away from a lifestyle that brings in hundreds and thousands of dollars a day without having something in hand to offer as an equal alternative. They say it is not practical to step to these dealers and ask them to give up something so lucrative without offering something to take its place.

My position is we use our experience to show that the negative alternatives outweigh the false sense of success they feel they have now. We must show the power of living a life that doesn't have the danger and stress of the streets. We must explain to them what is really at stake. Clarify why letting go of that fast money is worth the peace of not having to look over your shoulder constantly.

We must use the power of our testimony to help them come to the SANE/same conclusion. It must click in their heads so that they say; "Man, he/she comes from the same struggle I'm from. He/She is the real deal, not some stranger in a suit trying to tell me about things they haven't ever gone through."

The breakthrough is when they look at us, actually hear us, and then say to themselves, I want what he/she has.

There is no denying that drug dealing is a disease. It is a disease that requires no medication. All you need is a healthy dose of new thinking and a prescription for change. A change that increases your chances of living longer and having a 'No Fuss Funeral'

The 'No Fuss' Funeral

There is an exercise given in psychology classes and cognitive treatment programs where a person has to write their own eulogy. The assignment can range from writing what would be said if they died that day to what the eulogy would be if they died years from now. It is a very powerful exercise, and when done correctly, will have a profound impact on how a person views death and his or her own mortality.

I remember writing a poem when I was 17 years old and how I talked about my funeral being more crowded than the most popular nightclub. Women would be crying and waiting in line to walk by and kiss my cheek and my homies would stroll up in their only suit and tie to give my limp hand a pound.

I mentioned how people would blast my music from their cars as they drove to the cemetery. My homies would shoot their guns in the air like a 21-gun salute to recognize my status as a street soldier. In my perfect picture, the rain would start falling as the preacher says 'ashes to ashes and dust to dust.' The crowd would disperse slowly and I would be alone, again.

That poem is a clear picture of how I viewed my life at the time. I would later entitle my first album, 'Ghetto Heaven' and rap about an afterlife that held all of the intricacies of your typical hood. I was crazy. The irony is, that almost 20 years later, I could recite that poem or perform those songs in schools and detention centers across this country and still receive enthusiastic applause. I realize that one way to de-glorify that lifestyle is by exposing the lack of a legacy left by those who live it.

I am sure most of you could write a eulogy and use all kinds of flowery words or hardcore anecdotes about your life. So, let's go deeper. I challenge you, right now, to envision the type of funeral you would have if you died today. There are two choices: A sensational, drama-filled funeral or a 'No Fuss' funeral. **Let's go to the streets.**

In my early street-life years I attended some wild send offs. I've seen wives and step children fight in limousines. I've witnessed first cousins pull guns on each other. I've gone to funerals where the prominent emotions were anger and sadness. These are usually the funerals of those whose lives were cut short and their families are distraught as they scream out, why?

With the exception of innocent bystanders, we already know why. It is because they were living lives that exposed them to dangerous situations. They were dealing with people whose desperation out-ranked their own insanity. They were on corners where violence is expected and anticipated. They were at nightclubs that catered to gun-packing street thugs who care about money and image more than the sanctity of life. They were driving while intoxicated or with the thrill-seeking reckless abandon often seen in the movies and video games they love.

These are the funerals where families argue about whose fault it is or isn't and where insurance was not had, so a gravestone may be a long time coming. These are the funerals where the preacher or reverend becomes so frustrated with such premature and pointless death, that he forgets the grief of the family and instead of reading the eulogy, launches into an hour long sermon that admonishes and chastises this generation, the one before it, and everyone in attendance. This is your drama-filled funeral.

Lately, in my role as deacon at my church, I've attended the funerals of people who have passed away from natural causes in the twilight of their lives. Affectionately called 'home goings,' these services are serious but not overly solemn. Family members sincerely celebrate the life of their loved one. They share stories and tell jokes. They laugh and smile. They wipe away their few tears with a 'don't mind me' smile and a confession that they are going to miss the deceased–someone who lived a full life and left an imprint on the lives of all who knew him or her.

There are no fights amongst family, no overbearing mother, sister, wife, girlfriend, baby mama holding on to the casket wailing until her voice gives out. There is very little risk that someone may pull a gun out at good old Mr. Ralph Clayton's home going like they did at little Mook Mook's service. The preacher has no cause to stand up front and berate the mourners. He or she can stay on program and even allow a few extra people to come up and say some kind words about the departed.

The only distraction is when Deacon Williams' cell phone goes off, playing an unexpected hip-hop ringtone his grandson put on for him. He can't figure out how to turn it off and his wife slaps his arm for embarrassing her. (Note to Self: Create a class entitled Cell Phones for Seniors 101) I'm sorry. As I was saying, that is your 'No Fuss' funeral.

Accentuate the Positive

It is your attitude, not your aptitude,
that determines your altitude.
—Zig Ziglar

One of the surest ways of overcoming any addiction or compulsion is to let go of the negative beliefs that feed the demons inside of you. You have to embrace what is positive in your life. You cannot allow yourself to be pulled into that deep pit of self-pity or other peoples' mess. They say misery loves company, but I had a pastor who told me misery loves miserable company. It is not enough that you allow misery to hang out with you; misery wants you to be miserable too. **Let's go to school!**

In algebra, the rule for adding and subtracting negative and positive integers is that when you have a positive number and a negative number you are to subtract the smaller from the greater and then give the answer the sign of the higher number. For example $+4 + (-7)$ would become $-7-(4) = -3$ and since the greater number (-7) is negative, therefore the answer -3 will be negative. Another example would be $-2 + 5$, which becomes $5-2 = 3$. The 5 being greater and positive gives us a positive answer.

Apply that same formula to people. If a negative person clashes with a positive person and the positive person is greater, the results will be positive. This theory is so easy to prove it becomes fun. Think of any argument you've had with someone where they started yelling then you started yelling. They were hurt and angry, you were hurt and angry, and the end results were negative.

Imagine how different you feel when you don't allow yourself to get caught up in the back and forth yelling and screaming; you keep your voice even and your body language relaxed. You don't allow the vein in your neck or forehead to stick out. Even if the conversation doesn't end on a good note, if you remain positive and stand as the greater integer, you will feel positive throughout.

Here is a small **SANE Challenge** for you to try. The next time a person is yelling and screaming and reacting to you in an angry/negative way, just remain calm. Don't raise your voice and return the hostility. Keep a positive attitude all the way through. You will be the greater integer and I guarantee **your** results will be positive.

Is Y'all Hiring?

While we are discussing the power of being positive let us also look at the ways in which we turn our past pain into a positive future or as the old song said how we *'accentuate the positive.'* I could give you a host of examples, but I feel obligated to aim this one at the 700,000 prisoners scheduled to reenter society this year alone.

Have you ever been convicted of a felony?

That is the dreaded question on page two of your job application. Do you check *Yes* and then go on to the next question where it asks you to *'Please Explain?'* On the other hand, do you check the box that says *No* and pray they never find out. It is difficult to get a job today. Even more difficult when you have to admit to a potential employer you were a criminal and therefore a possible risk.

"I'm an ex felon. Nobody is going to hire me." I hear this from men and women and I will admit there is a disparity when it comes to hiring ex-offenders. So what do you do about it?

"I'm gonna do me. I'll go back to stealing or prostitution or selling drugs. And don't blame me because I did try to get a job."

Once again, there is a need to readjust your thinking. It is time for you to accentuate the positive of your negative situation.

When the application asks you to *'Please Explain'* you should do just that–explain. I know it seems like an invasion of privacy, but trust me the background check most of these companies run nowadays will read a lot worse than your own words. Dispute the thought that the question is intrusive. If you were about to hire a babysitter and he/she admitted to being a felon, you would want to know some of the details as well.

You must also realize not all companies give you the opportunity to explain. There are some industries where policies exist that bar an applicant for consideration if they have been convicted within a certain time. These companies look for a yes or no and the date(s) of offense. If your conviction isn't 5, 7, or 10 years old your application won't make it to the Human Resource Department.

Answer the question with honesty. Give the date of your conviction and the length of your prison stay. Let the employer know you accept responsibility for your actions and the consequences that followed. Here is the key–the accentuation. You then include a sentence or two telling how you used your prison experience to become a better person.

Have you've ever been convicted of a felony? Yes.

Please Explain: I was involved with drugs in my late teens and early twenties. I was convicted for drug related offenses in 1998. I was wrong. I made poor decisions and served 9 years to pay for them. I used my prison time to change my life. I earned my GED, took college courses, self-improvement classes and developed a strong work ethic that is evident in my employment history detailed above.

Something similar to that should ensure you receive an interview. You must be prepared to sell your redeeming qualities. Even if the interviewer doesn't mention the felony question you had better know he/she is weighing your answers, your body language, your tone of voice, even your smile. Remember to smile.

I taught a job skills class that focused on resume writing and interview skills for inmates who were soon to be released. It was a great class that provided the inmates with a professional resume to take out with them and the opportunity to participate in a Job Fair, which included local businesses, who were willing to hire ex felons.

Because of my love for drama, we did a lot of job interview role-playing. Allow me to share with you how some of the enacted interviews went down.

The Bad Interview

Employer–(Speaks into his desk intercom) Send in the next applicant.

Potential Employee–What's good, playa? (Strolls in and slouches down in the chair without waiting to be seated)

Employer–Good morning. Please, uh make yourself comfortable. Tell me a little about yourself.

Potential Employee–Uh, well you know. I'm a regular guy. I'm an Aries, youknowwhatImean? My favorite food is pizza. I like rap music. I used to rap. I can still flow a little, youknowwhatImean? I gotta couple kids. They go to school and stuff. I like sports, except golf and racecars; they're not really sports for real, youknowwhatImean? And uh, I …what else you want to know?

Employer–That is fine. Tell me, how did you hear about our company?

Potential Employee–Ray Ray told me y'all hiring. Yo, was he playin' me? Y'all is hiring right?

Employer–Ray who? Never mind. Yes, we are hiring. What type of experience do you have?

Potential Employee–I got all types of experience. I worked a couple of jobs. I got all types of experience at different stuff, youknowwhatImean?

Employer–Okay. It says hear you were convicted of a felony and spent some time in prison. Would you like to tell me about that?

Potential Employee–(Glares at the interviewer for a few seconds) I knew it. I knew it was coming. (Gets louder) Why you asking me about that? I did my time. If you don't want to hire me just say it. I could tell you weren't trying to hire me anyway. It's cause I got a record. Now if I would have lied on the application you'd be mad, youknowwhatImean. This is bulls#@%! (Storms out of office)

I may have exaggerated a little, but there are many job interviews that take place along those lines. Many of my fellow previously incarcerated persons do not realize they were being given a chance to prove themselves ready. They go into the interview on defense or even worse, with the attitude 'this is me, this is how I talk and how I am, what you see is what you get.'

Come on now. You don't call your potential boss, *playa'* and say *Y'all is* or *youknowwhatImean* at the end of every sentence and expect someone to hire you. If you're saying to yourself, "Why not? This is me." Then you need to rethink who you are and who you want to be. Ask yourself if you really want to be a part of the workforce, because you are going to have to make some changes. Let me give you an example of how to accentuate the positive.

Good interview
Employer–Why do you want to work here?

Potential Employee–Well Sir, I know you started this company with one product and two employees and in less than 10 years, you have become one of the biggest employers in this city. I admire your success and I believe I can be a benefit to the growth of this company.

Employer–Tell me a little about yourself.

Potential Employee–Well Sir, I am determined, focused, and self motivated. I am a hard worker. I take directions well. I am good with people. I work well with a team. And I would love to be a part of the culture here.

Employer–It says hear you were convicted of a felony and spent some time in prison. Would you like to tell me about that?

Potential Employee–Sure, not a problem. In my early twenties, I was convicted for selling drugs. I made some very poor decisions when I was younger and those choices led to me going to prison. I used my time inside to better myself. I received my GED and completed a few college courses. I learned to type 35 words per minute. I became a certified Physical Trainer. I learned to read, write and speak Spanish. I also have a folder with me filled with over 40 certificates I earned while incarcerated.

Please, tell me you see the difference in approach and attitude. That particular example is loosely based on my positive accentuations. I researched the company I was applying at so that I would be familiar with their history and mission. You can do the same even if it means mentioning the amount of lunch traffic a McDonalds receives during the week. You may not type 35 wpm, speak Spanish or have 40 certificates, but do mention the classes you did take and the certificates you did earn, whether it's two or twenty. The point is you have to present the positive you.

We can go even deeper in regards to letting your potential employer know about the Federal Bonding program, which makes them eligible to receive $5000 of fidelity insurance for a six-month period at no cost and with no deductible if they hire you. You can even elaborate on the fact that your being on parole is an additional motivator for you to be at work everyday; you can't afford to make a mistake.

Of course, there isn't any sure-fire way to guarantee you will be hired. It is hard for a college graduate to get a job today, let alone a convicted felon. You simply can't feed into the mentality that the world owes you because of what you've been through. Do not allow your present or past circumstances to justify you doing the wrong thing again.

It is easy to say, "I can't get a job because of my felonies, so I'm going to do whatever it takes to get by." Then you get caught doing 'whatever it takes', go back to prison and come out, with another felony and have to start from scratch again, which means you have another excuse to do "whatever it takes" again. Can we say insanity?

Let me share something deep with you. If you sold drugs or were part of a gang and if you survived prison; you are ahead of the curve in regards to becoming a success story. In my criminal lifestyle I learned how to run a business, I learned how to lead a team; I learned the law of supply and demand and skillful negotiation tactics. Prison equipped me to take direction and deal with high-pressure situations. I also learned how to adapt to diverse sects of people.

I have filtered and reapplied the education I gained while in my negative and crazy life into my positive and SANE life. The best teachers, preachers, and leaders graduate from a painful life. You are a survivor and you can do whatever you set your mind and heart to do. You increase your chances substantially by accentuating the positive and setting a new example. **Let's go back to school!**

Reeducation

At exactly which point do you start to realize, that life without knowledge is death in disguise.
—K.O.S (Knowledge of Self) Determination by Talib Kweli

For those of you who have made mistakes in the past and are ready to embrace the challenge of change, allow me to remind you that change is not comfortable. You have been doing things a certain way for so long that it often hurts to try to do things in a new way. You learn something for the first time and begin your education. You get information and you practice. You feel comfortable with it, you get good at it and it becomes a habit. If it is a habit of thought then it becomes an attitude.

When you enter into the military, you learn to make your bed in a way that differs from how you were taught as a child. You knew how to make a bed (education) but you had to learn a new way to make your bed due to your new environment (reeducation).

You learned how to drive at the age of 16 and you have been driving for over 20 years. You take a trip to Australia and low and behold, the cars have the steering wheel on the right side of the car and everyone drives on the left side of the road. You learned how to drive a long time ago (education), you must now learn how to drive the opposite way you were taught (reeducation).

Reeducation takes place when you receive new info. You practice and it feels uncomfortable. The uncomfortable feeling is called Cognitive Emotive Dissonance (CED). That is a fancy way of saying, "This doesn't feel right." You think about it for a little bit and you try again. Eventually, you start to become comfortable. You form a new habit. Reeducation has taken place.

Reeducation is a major step in setting a new example. You have to learn a new example in order to set one. You were taught your entire life that you have to do whatever it takes to survive. You have to be strong and never show signs of weakness. You were trained to keep your feelings bottled up and to not share your pain with other people. You learned to numb yourself with drugs and alcohol when you felt bad or when you didn't want to feel at all. You learned all sorts of negative behaviors to cope with the inadequacies you believe you possess. Although it may feel uncomfortable and you will have some cognitive emotive dissonance, you must accept the need for reeducation.

My reeducation decision was easy because I became accountable and admitted I was not doing a good job at managing my life. My biggest reeducation came in the form of learning (relearning) to let go of wanting to be in control. I didn't trust my circumstances in the hands of anyone but me. I finally let God take control of my life and I have relearned how to trust, not only God, but also the people He has blessed me to know.

You are at that fork in the road. One path leads to the continuation of drugs and alcohol, addiction, criminality, prison and early death. The other path is unknown to you but is filled with love and positive choices, success and a healthy long life. When put like that, the choice seems easy, but experience has taught us differently. The second path is going to be a struggle at first. There are going to be many difficult and uncomfortable moments. You will have to make decisions that are contradictory to everything you have learned in your life. But see the light that shines along that second path, you will not be alone and once reeducation has taken place you will have a new mindset, a new attitude and you will be a new example.

<u>SANE Challenges</u>

As you attempt to overcome the addictions and conquer the compulsions you must find a way to fill the void that will be left once you stop doing drugs and engaging in criminal acts. The same way addiction became your coping strategy for the void in your life you must now develop coping strategies to replace the addiction.

1. Create a list of things you did while in your addiction that added to your desire to use. These are called 'triggers' and can include things like going to a certain friend's house; listening to a certain song; going to bars and nightclubs; being in a mall or store; being bored; even certain smells can trigger a relapse into your addiction and/or criminality.

Now create a list of alternatives to doing the things that could trigger your relapse. These are your new coping strategies and can include things like going to a play or poetry café instead of a night club; reading and writing when bored; becoming active in a church and the community; playing sports or working out; spending time with your family; getting a mentor and becoming a mentor. You have to create your own list of things you enjoy, so that you can counter that urge to do things that promote your addictions and compulsions.

2. Create a Victim List. Make a list of every person you have hurt while in your insanity. Those you hurt physically and emotionally. Those you abused and neglected. Write the name of everyone you may have harmed in some kind of way by your actions and decisions. Then apologize to them. Some you can speak to in person, some may require a phone call, some you can write a letter. If they are no longer alive or if they are not available, write them a note of apology and read it out loud to yourself.

3. For those of you still building the positive you, please take as many classes and courses you can to increase your value as a person as well as in the work force.

PART 5

H.E.L.P.

HONESTY, EMPATHY, LOVE, PATIENCE

People must help one another; it is nature's law.
—Jean de La Fontaine

In order to become what God and your destiny has called you to be, you must first recognize you cannot do it alone. For every great person who has walked this earth, I guarantee at key points in their lives they had HELP. You have a difficult test to take, you ask for help. You want to lift heavier weights at the gym, you ask for help. You are a new parent, you ask for help.

You must be willing to give help as well as receive help. The key word is willing. Contrary to the above quote, do not believe for one second that you *have* to help. Helping others is a choice you make. The problem occurs when we choose not to help one another, when we go against our nature. We aren't going to go all the way to church with this one, but let us dip into Bible Study for a quick moment.

In 1 Corinthians Chapter 12, Paul talks about the different spiritual gifts we possess and how they all come from the same spirit. He then relates that we may represent different units/parts, but we are all of the same body. Some of us are good at preaching while others are good at teaching and others are good at healing. If we were all preachers, we would have no doctors and if we were all teachers, we would have no counselors. The body requires help from all of its members. If one member is harmed, we all suffer. If one member is honored, we all rejoice. There stands the foundation of who we are and whose spirit we share.

The biggest obstacle in achieving this successful harmony is pride. Pride prevents us from asking for help when we need it. I didn't believe an accomplishment could be great without someone to witness it. I considered it a hollow victory if there was no applause to follow it. I wanted people around, but only if I could control the circumstances. I had to be the leader and I never wanted to ask anything from my *supporters*. It has taken me a long time and a lot of self-inflicted pain to realize how important and valuable it is to have a strong support *system* rather than yes-man supporters. In essence, you have to have HELP. It became a new day when I realized I needed help.

There are many attitudes/virtues necessary for us to give and receive help. There is humility, willingness, gratitude, joy, self-control, caring, peace and faith to name a few. I will focus on the four attitudes I have grown to appreciate as being the core or heart of HELP.

These are Honesty, Empathy, Love and Patience. These four cover the basis for giving and receiving help. The help starts with you being willing to help yourself. **You** must be well in order to help anyone else. Let's go get help.

Honesty
The Foundation of Change

Honesty is the first chapter in the book of wisdom.
—Thomas Jefferson

You enter a corner store to buy a pack of chewing gum. There is a young high school student working the register. Her nametag says 'Hi, I'm Kelly.' She smiles and asks how you are doing as she rings you up. The price of your gum is .99 plus tax.

"That will be one dollar and five cents," she says nicely.

You hand her a five-dollar bill. She opens the register and gives you change back for a twenty. She smiles pleasantly, hands you 18 dollars and 95 cents, and says have a nice day.

What do you do? Think about it for a second. I have presented this scenario to many audiences, young and old. The debating that ensues always amazes me. Is it stealing if she gave you the money? Could it be a blessing from God? It is not my fault if she can't count. What would you do? Okay, hold on to that thought. Let's go deeper.

Kelly has been working there for only a week. She is trying to earn her own money to pay for her SAT test and her prom dress. When her boss comes in that evening and counts the drawer, he finds it short by almost 19 dollars. He has had employees steal from him before. He asks Kelly if she took the money and when she adamantly denies it, he becomes angry. Not only does he fire her, he calls the police and presses charges against her. All because you weren't honest enough to return the money.

That is a small example of the ripple effect created by one bad choice. Here is another.

You pay money for a prescription pill someone offers you at school. You have no idea what it is, you just want to feel good, stay awake and be one of the cool people. You take it, get dizzy on your way to your next class and pass out in the hallway. The nurse calls your parents, who leave work and come to pick you up from school. You continue to insist you are fine and that you haven't taken anything except a Benadryl the night before. Your parents want to take you to the emergency room to be sure. You say no, you just want something to eat and to get some rest.

Your father goes back to work and your mother stays home with you. After eating a sandwich and taking a brief nap at home, you start convulsing with seizures. You are rushed by ambulance to the emergency room where you have to have your stomach pumped in order to save your life. Your failure to be honest ends up costing thousands of dollars in hospital bills and more importantly almost cost your life.

Those are only two examples of why honesty is so important. Honesty is first because it is the foundation of all change. It is the starting point for anyone who desires to set a new example. You must take an honest look at who you are and why you have been repeating the same poisonous behavior time after time.

Honesty gives us the ability to confront and conquer the old behaviors and irrational thought processes. Honesty is what leads us to be 'self-accountable no excuses.' Honesty is what enables us to 'set a new example.' In essence, you cannot be SANE without being honest. I gave you examples of the adverse consequences of not being honest with others, but even worse is the failure to be honest with yourself.

"I'm tired of being in this rut." "I hate it here." "I don't want to keep going to prison." "I can't stand being in this relationship."

"I don't want to eat as much as I do." "I don't really like going out and partying all the time."

We make these statements, especially when we are feeling some of those adverse consequences from our actions. If we were to be honest we would say; "I am afraid to move from this spot." "I keep going to prison because I'm lazy, greedy and selfish." "I stay in this relationship because I don't believe I deserve better." "I eat in excess because I am depressed and eating makes me feel good." "I party and drink because I want to fit in and fitting in is a lot easier than being myself."

Honesty is the self-inventory that tells you what areas in your life need HELP. You must admit you are sick in order to receive the medicine needed to get better. There has to be a valid diagnosis in order to attack the disease. Those who fail to perform this candid self-analysis set themselves up to fail at their mission to change.

After you gain the courage and confidence to be honest with yourself, it becomes so much easier to be honest with others. You will develop an objective ability to call things as they are and HELP your friends and loved ones with genuine sincerity and a respected integrity. You will also gain what I call 'The Eye of a Ref.'

The Eye of a Ref

Be honest to those who are honest, and be also honest to those who are not honest. Thus honesty is attained.
—Lao Tzu

During my prison stay, I trained and became a certified basketball referee. I decided to take such an unpopular and risky assignment mainly because there was a need for impartial referees at the time. I had no idea what I was getting myself into, but as with most lessons learned, I walked away with a proficiency that has helped me in many areas of my life.

"Call it both ways!" That is a constant complaint amongst players, coaches and fans. I used to watch games and say it myself. If you call a foul on my team then you had better call a foul on the other team too. When our favorite team is involved, we have a bias, which prevents us from caring if the calling is good or bad; we just want it called both ways.

"Where's the foul ref?" We scream out when our player misses an easy layup.

"That wasn't a walk." We complain when our player is whistled for too many steps.

As a ref, you develop an eye that allows you to see so much more than what a typical spectator observes. I learned how to watch the players, the ball, and the out of bounds line all while running up and down the court. I have trained myself not to watch the game, but instead to watch every play as an isolated event. Then, call it as I see it.

When you are routing for a team you will more than likely have a partiality to what calls are good and bad. We do the exact same thing with our family and friends.

"I don't care if he's right or wrong, that's my brother and I got his back."

"She only stole a pack of cigarettes; they didn't have to arrest her like that."

Unless you have the eye of a ref, you cannot call it as you see it because deep down you want your team/family to win. Thus, your bias doesn't accept that your sister stealing leads to an arrest just as slamming the ball to the floor in frustration will earn you a delay of game; or a technical foul if you add profanity to your display of aggravation.

The eye of a ref allows you to call what you see with an unbiased integrity. The ref doesn't have a favorite team and he/she cares about the teams/family too much not to deal with them in honesty. You can use the eye of a ref to call it as you see it with your friends and family; whether it is talking to a friend about their body odor being offensive or sitting down with a family member to address their alcoholism/drug addiction. You should be able to call it both ways and as you see it. That type of honesty should permeate all areas of your life.

When you practice honesty, you develop a reputation of being a trustworthy person. You become the person most people seek out for HELP. You earn respect for your truthfulness and you inspire people to be honest as well. Without honesty, you cannot take any other steps towards changing who you are. You do not get rid of the 'Don't Blame Me' mentality, you are not released from your 'personal prisons,' you do not overcome the addiction or conquer the compulsions and you do not set a new example without first being honest enough to admit HELP is needed.

Empathy
(Can You Feel My Pain)

Remember those in prison as if you were their fellow prisoners, and those who are mistreated as if you yourselves were suffering.
—Hebrews 13:3 (NIV)

Empathy was another one of my seventh-grade vocabulary words. By definition, empathy is the capacity to share and understand another's emotions and feelings; often characterized as the ability to 'put oneself into another's shoes,' or in some way experience what the other person is feeling.

In treatment, the surface definition is to say empathy means to care because you understand. Add that to the aforementioned Wikipedia definition and we have empathy as caring because we understand what it is like in the other person's shoes.

As we elaborate on empathy, I want us to focus on the aspect of understanding what it is like in the other person's shoes. That is very important in our goal to give and receive HELP.

Your friend calls you up and tells you he/she lost her job. You have lost jobs in the past and you know how it feels. You can empathize with your friend's anger and fear and you can give help derived from your personal experience. You can give advice on filing for unemployment and change their budget while he/she is out of work. You have empathy because you have been in your friend's shoes.

Your classmate stands in the hall looking at the final-cut cheerleader list. She didn't make the team and she is fighting back tears as she scans the list one last time. You never tried out for cheerleading, but you share with her the times you weren't picked for basketball teams in your neighborhood pick-up league and how you didn't make band-front the first year you tried out. Your empathy is sincere because you have been in her shoes and you can tell her about trying harder next time and not allowing a team to define her worth. This is empathy at work and when it is genuine, it is often valuable.

There are many programs aimed at helping those who are struggling with drugs and alcohol, criminality, anger management, depression, reentry for formerly incarcerated people and more.

Many of these programs fail for one reason alone–the inability to relate to the pain and suffering of those who the programs are designed to help. The inability to put one's self in those types of shoes.

Imagine a Parenting Class teacher who doesn't have children, an AA Sponsor who has never had a drink, or a Reentry counselor who has never been to prison. Some things need to be experienced in order to empathize with a person in that particular struggle.

Please don't misunderstand me. I am not saying you have to have gone to prison to help someone who is in prison or coming home from prison. You do not have to sell drugs to empathize with a drug dealer. What I am saying is there are certain emotions involved and evolved from those experiences that you can't understand and therefore, put on those shoes. If you have never felt like the world owed you something because of what you have endured, it will be difficult for you to empathize and encourage someone who feels that way.

I have a friend who recently came home after spending over 16 years in prison. He called me up late in the evening frustrated because he couldn't figure out how to reply to an email he received. His 11-year-old daughter had helped him before and he was too ashamed to admit he still didn't understand. I felt his pain. I could empathize with him. Sure, his wife and his daughter may understand his frustration as well, but it is not the same as talking with someone he knows was in his shoes.

I shared with him how I felt when I was in the Halfway House and went to the Wal-Mart to apply for a job and they sent me to a self-serve computer application booth. I told him how I stared at the computer for 10 minutes trying to gather enough courage to try. He knew that I knew what he was feeling. We laughed at ourselves for a minute (the mutual empathy allows for some self-deprecation), and then I walked him through the email process several times until he felt comfortable with it. That is empathy at work.

Empathy is also very instrumental in promoting growth in our quest to become better people. I remember when I was in my denial how I didn't want to be compared to someone who was addicted to cocaine, crack, heroin or methamphetamines. I believed my addictions–drinking and smoking weed–were only social vices that helped me deal with the pressure of being a drug dealer. In my mind, they were fiends and I wasn't like 'them.'

As I sat in treatment groups and heard 'them' share their thoughts and feelings about the regrettable things they did while in their sickness, I could reflect and relate to doing some of the same foolish things, while in my sickness. Our addictions may have been different, but we were able to empathize with the similar outcomes. We could also walk in each other's shoes when it came to discussing the negative baggage we were carrying.

I also sat across from Wall Street investors and Hedge Fund managers who were millionaires and listened to them describe the inadequacies they felt from not having a father or the pressure they were under to become successful. These rich, white men were talking about my feelings and it shocked me to the core. I realized that my suffering, mistakes and negative thoughts were not unique to me. I didn't have a monopoly on poverty, pain or prison and I could no longer rationalize my refusal to share or empathize with the excuse, 'nobody could feel my pain or walk in my shoes.'

In order to give and receive HELP, you must have empathy. You will be tested in your resolve to assist those who are in an earlier stage of their change. I deal with men, women and children who have one foot in the streets and one foot in the church. I force myself to remember when I was still adapting to change. I don't curse or drink or smoke anymore, but I used to and I empathize with those who still do. When you have empathy, you learn how to foster and encourage change without being judgmental. You learn how to be the example you are setting while remembering the examples you have overcome.

Love
(The Greatest of these...)

This is my commandment, that ye love one another, even as I have loved you.
—John 15:12

Love is the only force capable of transforming an enemy into friend.
—Dr. Martin Luther King JR

Men and women lay hurt in the street or in hospital waiting rooms, people just look at them, and walk by. Students are assaulting teachers and shooting other students and teachers in the schools. Young people are killing themselves and broadcasting it over the internet. Children are abused, neglected, and dying from that abuse and neglect. Men and women are walking into churches, restaurants and businesses and shooting as many people as they can. Children are being abducted and murdered. People are murdering their families and then committing suicide. There are kidnappings, slave trading, arsons, and political sex scandals.

This country has a culture of violence that covers the spectrum from fighting and shooting to stabbings and decapitations.

There is a lack of respect for the value of human life and a total disregard for the well-being of our fellow man. The reason this world is in such dire need of revival is because there is a need for love. *"What the world needs now is love... sweet love."*

Although, I have listed Honesty first and as the foundation of change, love is the heart of HELP. When you have love, you have no choice but to be honest with yourself and others. Love instills an instant empathy for others and provides a compassion that negates the hatred that breeds the violence, neglect and abuse mentioned throughout this book. When you have love, you have an automatic patience that allows you to wait on those you love to reach their breaking point and receive their breakthrough in the same manner you wait on the Lord.

With love, we are able to remain consistent with our theme of looking into the mirror and starting with ourselves. We must possess self-love. When you have self-love, you do not do hateful or harmful things to yourself.

I love me some me. I love myself. That is the attitude you must adopt. Go ahead and say it out loud. I LOVE ME! I love myself too much to risk my life having unprotected sex with someone I just met. I love myself too much to get involved with drugs. I love myself too much to join a gang. I love myself too much to be with someone who wants to beat on me. I love myself too much to drop out of school. I love myself too much to keep drinking everyday. I love myself too much to give up on me.

Let's talk for a brief minute about Agape love. That is the Biblical love, defined as a divine, unconditional, self-sacrificing, active, volitional, and thoughtful love. It is also referred to as charity or love in action. Jesus referred to this love when he said:

Love (agapao) the Lord your God with all your heart and with all your soul and with all your mind.' This is the first and greatest commandment. And the second is like it: 'Love (agapao) your neighbor as yourself.' All the Law and the Prophets hang on these two commandments."

Mathew 22:37-40

Agape love is what I call 'ultimate love.' You really have to experience some healing in your life in order to have Agape love. You don't bring the pain from a past relationship into a new relationship if you have Agape love. You don't walk past a stranger on the street with his hand extended for 'a little change' when you have Agape love. It is hard to become angry when you have this ultimate love and you feel the pain of the entire human race when you have Agape love. That is why we must love with action. We love with deeds that empower, teach, and ultimately change the bad things of this world to good.

Imagine for a second, what it could be like if we allowed the love, faith and trust we have in God and the recollection of all He has carried us through, guide us in all of our decision making. Let us picture what the world could be like if we really stayed true to that commandment to love one another as brothers, to be courteous and kind and to love as Jesus loved us. Oh what a world it would be.

When you have that real and ultimate love, you love as if you've never been hurt and as if tomorrow may not come. Agape love isn't exclusive to your spouse, lover or children; it is for your fellow man as a whole. There are people who have hurt you and done things to you that seem unpardonable, but when you have Agape love, you will not have the bitterness, anger, hatred, and all of the other emotions that cloud your spirit and make it hard for you to grow and progress and become the person you are called to be. Agape love brings forgiveness and when you have Agape love, you involuntarily set a new example.

Wait for your Soul Mate

For it was not into my ear you whispered, but into my heart. It was not my lips you kissed, but my soul.
—Judy Garland

Please allow me to digress for a minute. I would be remiss only to speak of love in regards to self-love and its brotherly (Agape) love context. One of the major components of my transition stems from the love I was blessed with in the form of my soul mate. I know how important it is to have a partner who sees you for who you are and consistently encourages you to become who you are supposed to be. Thus, if you will bear with me for a few paragraphs I will talk to you about a new example of an old-fashioned love.

First of all, let me make clear what you are about to read comes from a grown man. You have read enough so far to know my history. You know my background. I am not ashamed to write about love and spending my life with the one person who was made to love me the way I deserve to be loved. For you young adults reading this book, I pray that you have heard this before. If not, let me be the first to tell you; there is nothing wrong with wanting to be in love and saving yourself for the person who puts a ring on your finger and declares their love for you in front of God and all who wish to witness such a great commitment. Open your heart and let us go to the soul.

Many people are giving up on their destiny. Men and women alike no longer believe in soul mates. They consider the search for a soul mate a fruitless, mythical endeavor meant only for hopeless romantics. Allow me to elaborate on the legitimacy of soul mates and why searching is never necessary.

As with everything, it begins spiritually. Soul mates love each other with the faith that God has ordained their love. Soul mates recognize they are part of the same essence and therefore, are never afraid to give their all to their partner. They are blessed with an honesty that encourages them to tell each other any and everything. Soul mates open up to each other in the same uninhibited way one opens up in their private prayers to God.

This doesn't entail soul mates are perfect people with perfect loves. Soul mates are not perfect, but they know how to look past the imperfections of their partner. They disagree, argue, and raise their voices in passionate displays of disappointment. Yet, soul mates seldom separate on bad terms. They have learned that living without one another is a lot more painful than the temporary hurt of some disagreement.

The testing ground for Soul mates is their ability to communicate. I am talking deeper than that uncanny ability to finish each other's sentences. Soul mates have a way of communicating without words. They have certain looks that sing songs. They have smiles that say, "Come here, please" and eyewinks that say, "I'll take care of it." They even have frowns that plead, "I need better." Soul mates can cuddle together and have a complete conversation in silence.

Soul mates are two people who are destined to love one another. They are drawn together by an energy that crosses continents and oceans, yet usually has only to skip over a few backyards. Soul mates are best friends who grow to be lovers. Soul mates are lovers who grow to be best friends. Soul mates can weather any storm together and no matter how independent or self-reliant a person is; once they have found their soul mate, they will always feel incomplete without them.

Your soul mate is that person who you can't stay angry with; the person you miss without knowing why; the person who can change your climate whenever they're around. Your soul mate is the person who God intended to love you the way He meant love to be.

I am in love with my soul mate. I have such a beautiful soul mate story and although I won't go into it right here, please feel free to ask me about it when you see me in person. I will share this much with you; my soul mate told me she is my rib. She said she came from me and that it is only right she return to her rightful position–at my side, protecting my heart.

Did I have to search for her? No. I simply had to open my eyes and see that the woman in front of me was a part of me. That she is indeed my soul mate. See, soul mates believe in each other which means they believe in soul mates; which means they believe in love.

Patience... (More than a virtue)

Patience and fortitude conquer all things.
—Ralph Waldo Emerson

And let patience have its perfect work, that ye may be perfect and entire, lacking in nothing.
—James 1: 4

Change does not come overnight. You have to allow yourself the room to transition, to learn and relearn. Many people are fond of quoting how they "waited patiently on the Lord." Well, you should have waited patiently, especially after how long the Lord had to wait for you. I can tell you from experience, your evolution into a SANE individual will bring a longing for more feelings of positivity.

You thirst for the change to get deeper and deeper within you, so you can feel better and better. You have to have patience in order to avoid the disappointment of change not coming fast enough... for you. Again, the patience you achieve for yourself will make it easier to be patient with others.

You have a loved one who is going through some serious issues and trying hard to take you with them. You've been honest with them about their behavior and how you feel because of their behavior. You showed empathy by reflecting back on your own struggles. You shared with them how you could relate and 'feel' their pain. And you loved them. You forgave them for all they had done to hurt you and you loved them with that Agape love we spoke about earlier. You offer to HELP by any means within your power. And the next day this loved one does the same thing again.

You want to give up. You are tired of going through the same mess. I have been there and I understand. The key is making sure you draw a line between being patient and being an enabler. See, enabling someone to continue down a destructive path is very different from waiting for a person to see the light and feel the heat and accept positive change.

I can visit you at rehab and assure you I will be there for you when you get out, but I am not going to lend you 15 dollars at three o'clock in the morning. I can berate and chastise you ten times a week about your criminal activities, but if I also allow you to give me money or take me out with the money you gain from those illegal acts, I enable you to view my acceptance of your gifts as acceptance of your criminal exploits.

Patience entails having endurance, persistence, tolerance and fortitude. It shouldn't matter whether you are dealing with a coworker, a parent or a child; if you are trying to HELP them, you must use patience. The friend I mentioned earlier who needed help with the computer ended up calling me at least 10-15 times for more help and I helped him with joy in my heart (most of the time) because I know he needed my patience just as I often need the patience of others.

Patience is so much more than a virtue. Picture your first day in your new home with your new spouse and imagine the patience that will be required as you learn about each other's little quirks. Think of the birth of your first child; how patient you must be as you learn to care for another little soul who depends on you for so much.

Now, imagine your child giving a graduation speech and saying, "I have to thank my mom and dad for never giving up on me and for having patience as I went through the uncertain phases of my life." Patience is mandatory in our desire to give HELP.

Let me also touch on how the lack of patience is affecting the education of our children. We bought our 13 year old a Rubik's Cube as a stocking stuffer for Christmas. She lost interest in it after a few hours and gave it to our 7 year old. He struggled with it for a few hours and then attempted to remove the stickers in order to solve the puzzle. When I asked him why he was peeling away the stickers, he said, "I know what it should look like but it's taking too long to solve." That is when I realized he probably feels the same way about learning economics and fractions in school.

Children today play video games that are much more advanced than the ones I played in the 80's and certainly more advanced then the board games of the Baby Boomer generation. My youngest son has played the John Madden video football games for the past few years and can move his little fingers and thumbs fast as lightning to scroll through 3-4, 4-3 and nickel defenses with monster blitzes. He can also pick an offensive shotgun formation with five receivers running different routes all calling for an exact timing in order for him to complete the pass. All of this happens in the 5 to 12 seconds it takes to decide what play to use and he still has the option to audible the play after all of that. His sisters are just as fast with their fingers and thumbs due to the excessive amount of phone texting they do on a daily basis.

My child then goes to school and the teacher is at the board writing with chalk or a dry erase marker and the teacher is writing so slow, my son can anticipate not only what he/she is going to write but solve the problem as well. When the teacher is ready to ask the question, he blurts out the answer and gets a warning for speaking out of turn. Then as he is waiting for the teacher to explain the formula for the problem; he gets bored, he fidgets around, he gets out of his seat and gets in trouble.

He's not thinking about math anymore. The math problem was easy and it is over. He's worried about how long he will have to go without playing his PSP video game for getting in trouble.

The attention span of our children shadows the speed of the world today, namely the computer speeds, cell phones and video games. The children are accustomed to the fast pace of their games and their lack of patience has spilled over into the other areas of their lives. Our children are being diagnosed with ADD and ADHD because they are frustrated by how fast they can think versus how slow the world is turning. Our children are learning in gigabytes now and we have to make the adjustments if we are to keep up with them.

We as parents and teachers must do a better job of recognizing the significance of technology as well as finding a compromise to make sure our children maintain a healthy patience in their lives. Teachers can alter their teaching pace and include games and computers to help them teach. As parents, we need to play games with our children that also require patience to avoid the frustration they will feel when they aren't catching on to calculus right away. Teach your child to play chess and checkers. Play Scrabble and Monopoly. Take a deck of cards and turn them all face down and play Memory.

I am not in any way encouraging the slowing down of the learning process or asking teachers to turn over the reins to computers. I am simply making an observation of the patience that is lacking in our younger generation and how detrimental it could be to their futures. They will need to be quick thinkers and know how to react quickly to the constant change of what the world demands, but they must also have the patience to think and weigh the several outcomes of their decision-making, they must have the patience to work for their desired outcomes and not believe everything should come fast and easy.

I will also take a moment to emphasize patience in regards to our young children wanting to grow up too fast. You have 11, 12, and 13 year olds having sex and having babies. My 13 year old was honest enough to admit that many girls her age like the attention from boys. I remember as an adolescent feeling the same way about girls. We as the middle generation must play are part in providing a healthy attention so that our future generation doesn't crave the negative attention that comes with premature relationships.

Let me talk to you middle-school students for a minute. Please hear me on this. You are special. And you have so much time ahead of you to worry about boyfriends or girlfriends. You will go on dates to the movies and to dances. You will fall in love and someone will love you in return. You may have your heart broken and you might break someone's heart. But right now, you must be confident enough to be a young person. You need to focus on being a great student and if you want more attention, get involved in sports, music, theatre, or community service.

When your peers are talking about having a boyfriend/ girlfriend, you have to step away from the crowd and say that is 'Not Cool.' When your peers are talking about talking dirty on the phone or the computer or 'sexting' and using their phone to send nude pictures to their boyfriend or girlfriend, you need to say; 'Not Cool.' When these friends are boasting about having sex, you need to say to yourself and to them, "that is 'Not Cool'."

I understand how difficult it is being a teenager today. I realize you have pressure coming at you from so many different angles that it is overwhelming at times. Many of you have already found joy, acceptance and a sense of love from giving yourself to another. I want you to understand you are still worthy of being a beautiful, intelligent, successful and SANE young person.

You have to change how you think. You have to look into that mirror and see who you are and who you can become. You have to have the confidence to tell yourself you are beautiful and you don't need that confirmation from anyone else. You don't need to have sex in order to be loved. You love yourself enough to say I am worth the wait and if someone wants to be with me than they better have patience because right now I am setting a new example. You can do it!

Communication Is the Key

When you know something, say what you know. When you don't know something, say that you don't know. That is knowledge.
—Kung Fu Tzu (Confucius)

In order to be successful in any situation, it is imperative you have effective communication. Whether it is a conversation with you parents, dealing with a bully at school, talking to a teacher or your boss at work, you want to be able to communicate your wants in an effectual manner. You have to be honest, empathetic, loving and patient. You must be confident without being arrogant and you must be clear and concise in what you want. In other words, you must be assertive.

There are four styles of communication: Assertive, Aggressive, Passive, or Passive-Aggressive. You must first identify what style you use. More than likely, you probably use a combination of all four depending on the situation. But there is one you are most comfortable with and that one is what most people would identify as your primary style of communication.

'*You are important but I am not.*' This is the motto of the **Passive** communicator. Your main objective is to avoid conflict and you comply with what most people ask of you and just go with the flow. You ask very little questions and try your best not to rock the boat. Others see you as a push over or become frustrated when dealing with you. You sacrifice honesty in an effort to please others. Your self-esteem is very low and you are a volcano waiting to explode.

'*I am important, but you are not.*' This is the motto of the **Aggressive** communicator. You specialize in manipulation. You get your way by any means necessary. You use guilt, hurt, anger and control tactics to manipulate others. You are forceful and brutally honest. Others see you as a bully and feel hurt, angry and distrustful around you. Your self-esteem is low and you believe you must attack first in order to protect yourself.

'*I am important, you are not, but I don't want you to know it.*' This is the motto of the **Passive-Aggressive** communicator. You combine the first two styles by trying to manipulate in an indirect manner. You are sneaky and sarcastic. You appear honest, but your intentions are to get your own way. Others feel confused around you and don't know who you are or what to expect. Your self-esteem is low; you want to fight for your respect, but only if nobody knows you are fighting.

'*I am important and you are important.*' This is the motto of the **Assertive** communicator. This style of communication should be your aim in all of your relationships. You are assertive when your self-esteem is high. You believe in a win–win situation. You care about your relationships so you are direct and honest. You respect others but refuse to compromise your values for someone else to obtain their goal.

Notice how the first three styles of communication all lack strong self esteem. Once again, we find the power of setting a new example, in this case being an assertive communicator, hinges on our beliefs, love and respect of self. You have to look into the mirror again and resolve to see yourself as someone other people will trust, respect, love and want to give HELP to and seek HELP from.

The most important part of communication is listening. People can speak 100–175 words per minute, but they can listen intelligently at 600–800 words per minute. The typical mindset is to communicate and get 'what I want.' I have to talk until someone understands what I am trying to get or do. We fail to give and receive HELP when we fail to listen in our communication. How can I HELP you if I haven't taken the time to listen to what is wrong and how can you HELP me if you don't listen to what I am telling you.

We have to learn how to be active listeners. We must get rid of the biases that we use to validate our desire to control or dominate the conversation. We have to accept the fact that we cannot learn without being able to listen. Great communication requires a receiver and a sender. If you constantly send and don't receive you are participating in a monologue and not a dialogue. That is not listening. That is not communication.

I want you to think about how your mind works when you are involved in a discussion. If you are thinking of what you are going to say next rather than listening to what is being said, that is not communicating. If you are answering questions with questions; that is not communicating. If you are finishing the other person's sentences; that is not communicating. If you are daydreaming while the other person is speaking, that is not communicating. If you constantly change the subject to what you want to talk about; that is not listening and that is not communicating.

It will be almost impossible for you to help someone if your communication style is lacking and your listening skills are missing. You must include the ability to communicate assertively as a prerequisite for changing who you are and becoming SANE.

T.I.C. (The Inner Conversation)

If you realized how powerful your thoughts are, you would never think a negative thought.
—Peace Pilgrim

When I was younger, I had a friend who had a nervous tic. His mouth would twitch; he would wink his eye and shrug his right shoulder involuntarily. He did it all the time and I remember teasing him and then feeling sorry for him when others teased him. I asked him one day if it hurt and when he told me no, I asked him what it feels like. He said, "I think my body just reacts to all of the thoughts I have in my mind. Every time I think of something it shows in my tic."

Wow! It took me many years to realize how much wisdom was shared with me that day from the mind of an eight-year-old who had an overflow of self-esteem to go with his tic. I now believe we all have a tic. It may not show on the outside like my friend, but we all have thoughts that make up a cognitive communication within ourselves. It is our TIC or The Inner Conversation. We have a self-talk that I mentioned in the 'Easy as ABC' chapter. The self-talk, TIC, is used to counter the negative thoughts/beliefs we have, so that we can feel the way we want to feel. The inner conversation is our most important communication because it teaches us to talk to and listen to ourselves.

If I admit I talk to myself, would you think I am crazy or not sane? I hope not. By now, you should be able to recognize the benefits of having a healthy inner conversation. You must learn to use your TIC to affirm and reaffirm who you are and why you should make the right choices. Use your TIC to tell yourself you are not a loser. Use your TIC to affirm your intelligence and your beauty and your worth and your strength. If you tell yourself you are going to do great in the school play or on the job, more than likely you will do great. You are what you think and you will feel what you tell yourself to feel.

Isn't that a beautiful thing? That is the power you have and you should never give that power to someone else. When you allow someone or something to dictate how you feel, you give away your power. Do not do it! Use your TIC and talk to yourself whenever you feel pressure to do something that doesn't represent the example you want to set. Find or create affirmations to say to yourself. For example, I am free! I deserve better! I am loved! I am not tired! I am relaxed! I have all that I need! I am healthy! I am successful. Everything will be all right!

The Inner Conversation is your ability to communicate positive influence on your life. When you have mastered the art of not only talking to yourself, but also listening and hearing yourself, you become the wonderful example of someone who is able to HELP others because you have mastered how to HELP yourself.

SANE Challenges

1. Establish a day of service for yourself and your family. A day where you commit to helping with public service projects such as homeless shelters, beautification projects, community outreach and educational workshops, etc… You can do this once a year, once a month or eventually once a week.

2. I personally challenge you to create your own 'I love you Day.' Instead of sending a forwarded email or text message go to every contact in your phone and email address book and call or send each person a message informing him or her that you love them. Take the time to actually type/text/call them personally by name. Again, you can do this as often as you would like. If you are one of those people who need a start date, how about the first weekend in August. The world needs to see more love; set a new example.

PART 6

PERSONAL SOUNDTRACKS

Music is the shorthand of emotion.
—Leo Tolstoy

There is an African Folktale that says when a child is born a song is created specifically for that child. It is a song for them to identify with throughout their lives. It is played and sung for them to celebrate accomplishments as well as when they depart from the correct path. If the child/adult does something negative, the rest of the village would sing and play their song to them as encouragement to remember who they are and where they come from.

I love that imagery because it explains how music can resonate within one's soul. Have you ever heard a beat that compels you to get up and move? Have you ever heard someone sing a high note that literally sends chills through your body? You get goose bumps and your hair stands up. It can be a high note or the witty wordplay of a metaphor or just a simple display of words that hit home to you and what you're going through. You don't even have to understand the language; the passion, joy and pain comes through in a universal communication. That is the power of music.

Music has always been a big part of the tapestry of our lives. Our lives have a soundtrack and there are different songs for the different phases of our lives. You have music you clean up to, music you get dressed to, music to drive to, and music you break up to and make up to. There are songs that when you hear them you automatically flash back to a certain time in your life.

My father in law, Doug Smallwood hears *'Back To The World'* by Curtis Mayfield and flashes back to the Vietnam Era. He remembers being overseas in the early 70's, waiting to return to the USA.

"I came home and found the country I fought for, not only didn't care about our sacrifices but rewarded us returning veterans with less benefits, no jobs and a stigma of failure to have to deal with. All of this because of an unpopular war whose desired outcome was un-attainable from the beginning! No wonder so many of us from that era turned to drugs, which has ultimately impacted the generation that followed."

My Aunt Leenita Johnson hears James Brown's *'Say It Loud– I'm Black and I'm Proud'* and remembers an era of newfound pride in her race and her womanhood.

"I remember that feeling of pride in being black. We as a black people could express ourselves so freely through our music, our poetry, our art and even in our dress. Black women were viewed as Nubian Queens; all shades of blackness were celebrated; from Angela Davis to Cicely Tyson. There were the Black Panthers, NAACP, and the Civil Rights Movement. It was a defining time; recognizing who God had created me to be and knowing I was special. I was black and proud."

My Aunt Marva Queen hears *'God Loves You'* by the Canton Spirituals and flashes back to an era of self loathing and depression. She hears this song from her personal soundtrack and remembers how it helped her get through.

"It was a point in my life when I was overweight, depressed, and very lonely. I was angry and I blamed myself for losing my husband to other women. The words of this song made me realize that if my husband didn't really love me for who I was, it was ok. The main man in my life (God) brought me through. HE was the only one I needed to love me. That song brought me BACK!"

My wife, Lenia Queen hears *'The Arms of the One Who Loves You'* by Xscape and remembers the comforting confidence it provided her when I was not ready to give her my all.

"I think back to one of the times me and my husband had parted ways in our dating days. Even when we were apart I knew it wasn't for long. Something in my heart knew I was going to be his wife. I woke up one night hearing this song and watching the video and I knew that the words being sung were coming from the secret diary of my heart."

There are many examples of how varied and reflective your personal soundtrack can be. My Aunt Gert hears *'American Pie'* by Don Mclean and recalls a time of lost innocence and freedom to start anew. My Aunt Donna hears *'Wildflower'* by New Birth and remembers that song speaking to her heart and giving a definition of the woman she was during that time.

My friend Trina Traynham hears *'Black Butterfly'* By Denise Williams and flashes back to her eighth-grade graduation and how that song gave her the inspiration to spread her wings and prepare to grow up and experience life. My friend Jack O'Donnell hears *'Paradise by the Dashboard Light'* by Meatloaf and flashes back to high school, cars and girls and commitment issues he has struggled with throughout most of his relationships.

Are you getting the idea? Do you see how impactful music has been on our lives? Who can say they don't think of a certain time when they hear *'What's Going On'* by Marvin Gaye, *'At Last'* by Etta James, or *'A Change is Going to Come'* by Sam Cooke. Who doesn't have a Luther Vandross song in their personal soundtrack?

You can have songs from eras when you weren't alive be part of your personal soundtrack, mainly because each era will have someone singing and addressing some of the same issues every generation will face.

Aretha Franklin, Patti Labelle and Diana Ross were to my mother what Whitney Houston, Mariah Carey and Mary J Blige were to me and what Keyshia Cole, Alicia Keys and Beyonce are to my children. James Brown was to my father what Michael Jackson was to me and what Usher and Chris Brown are to my children.

Because of the similarities and influences of these artists on each other, it becomes natural for our personal soundtracks to have a multi-generational sound. My parents introduced me to Stevie Wonder I introduced them to R Kelly. They had the Ojays and Eddie Levert; I had his sons Gerald and Sean. They put me on to the Temptations and Wham and I showed them New Edition, Jodeci and Boys To Men.

I consider myself a music connoisseur. I have so many songs on my personal soundtrack I could fill up many iPods and MP3 players. But Hip-hop is my first love and I am a child of the Hip-hop culture.

I remember attending High School dances when I was only 13 and hearing Run DMC, LL Cool J and Slick Rick. I remember going to the skating rink and doing the fast skate to 'It Takes Two' by Robb Base. I flash back to Bethea's Arcade when I hear 'Friends' by Whodini. I recall African beads and medallions and my era of becoming socially conscious when I hear Public Enemy's 'It Takes a Nation of Millions to Hold Us Back' and Boogie Down Productions 'Criminal Minded.'

I recall having a personal soundtrack for my weed smoking days. I had Method Man and Redman's 'How High' and 'I Got Five on It' by the Luniz. Not much different than my parent's generation listening to 'Mary Jane' by Rick James and my grand parents listening to Cab Calloway's 'Reefer Man.'

As an aspiring rapper in my own right, I loved the lyrical styles of Kool G Rapp, Big Daddy Kane, Rakim, Nas, Biggie Smalls and Jay Z. When the late B.I.G. came out with 'Juicy' and said *"It was all a dream/ I Used to read Word Up magazine/ Salt and Peppa and Heavy D up in the limousine."* I could relate to that same dream and for him to put out '10 Crack Commandments,' well, that spoke to my reality.

When NWA described the 'Dopeman' and the 'Gangsta, Gangsta;' when Tupac talked about 'Brenda's Got a Baby' and being 'Trapped' or 'Violent' and feeling like 'Me Against the World' I can recall the connection that was made within my consciousness. It felt as if someone who I had never met was giving voice to the pain and suffering I either felt or saw everyday. I was able to legitimize my beefs with my surroundings and learn how other young men and women in other/similar poor circumstances were handling their lot in life.

Hip Hop Hoo-ray... Today

Stressing how hardcore and real she is, she was really the realest before she got into showbiz
—'I Used To Love Her,' by Common Sense

MCing, DJing, Break Dancing and Graffiti. From sampled break beats to live bands. From the Budweiser Super Fest and Fresh Fest to Sold-out Arenas all over the world. Hip-hop is over 30 years old and more popular than ever, but like a child from the ghetto who inherits a fortune and then travels the world, its attitude has changed.

Hip-hop was once fresh and fun. MCs were sidekicks to DJs and focused on getting the crowd excited. Lyrics were creative and catchy, stylish and humorous. Songs like 'Parents Don't Understand' and 'Girls Aren't Nothing but Trouble' by Jazzy Jeff and the fresh Prince (Will Smith) poked fun at being a teenager. Hip-hop was also political and informative in its infancy. KRS-One called himself the Teacher and he did educate with songs like 'You Must Learn' and 'My Philosophy.' Melle Mel delivered 'The Message' and public Enemy said 'Fight the Power.'

The Fat Boys wanted 'All You Can Eat' and Run DMC bragged about their favorite sneaker on 'My Adidas.' Eventually hip-hop began to worship things a little more expensive. 'All About the Benjamins' by Sean 'P Diddy' Combs and the Bad Boy camp was in reference to hundred dollar bills which have Benjamin Franklin's face on them. 'Bling Bling' by the cash Money Millionaires was in praise of the diamonds they wore and Lil Wayne's 'A Milli' is a boastful sonnet about being a young millionaire.

Today, Hip-hop has become a multi *billion* dollar-a-year industry. The Hip-hop Culture has exploded across the globe. The youth of Japan, France, Amsterdam and South Africa, to name a few, wear baggy Hip-hop clothing and although many can barely speak the English language, they can quote 50 Cent's 'In Da Club' word-for-word.

Break dancing, which was once stereotyped as an urban craze, is now seen on Broadway and as a featured category in national dance competitions. Graffiti was once illegal and looked at with disdain as an eyesore on subway trains, buses and abandoned buildings. Graffiti artists are now commissioned to do murals and their work can be seen and sold in art galleries all over the world. Hip-hop makes up over 40 percent of the top 40-radio format and DJs now host number one radio shows all over the world. Hip-hop artists own luxury cars and live in expensive homes displayed on television shows like MTV Cribs.

Today Hip-hop has grown from a fun-filled block party to a worldwide Mardi gras. I share with you this brief foot note from my version of Hip-hop 101 as a preface to what I am about to share in regards to my own personal soundtrack. I want you to understand why I am so passionate about the evolution of my personal soundtrack.

I was rappin' when I was 11 years old. I would battle eighth graders when I was in sixth grade. I remember my father giving me 20 dollars to buy a pair of sneakers and he said I could keep the change as long as I got a pair of sneakers. I bought a pair of Converses for $1.99 from Becks and used the change to get a name belt with my MC name... ACE.

I have performed for thousands in talent shows, street fairs and nightclubs since I was 15 years old. I have done concerts where the headliners were Rock and Roll acts and the crowds booed when they saw five young black guys with baggy pants and designs in their high top fades. I have stopped the music and free styled a cappella in order to prove I had lyrical flow.

I have performed in an all women's state prison where fights broke out after we did the Bobby Brown 'No Humping Around' grind on the ground. I have driven from Harrisburg to Philadelphia on a Wednesday afternoon to hear my song played on Power 99 FM. I have promoted successful album release parties/concerts and had considerable cassette and cd sales.

When I was younger, my personal soundtrack was a blend of KRS One's 'Love's Gonna Get Cha," and Slick Rick's 'Hey Young World.' I lived both lifestyles and reaped the rewards and consequences that came with them. I was an R&B aficionado as well and I had plenty of 120-minute 'Slow Jam' cassettes to woo young ladies.

In my criminal element, I rode to the sounds of Ice Cube, Nas, Tupac, Biggie and Jay Z. Ice Cube talked about his 'Summer Vacation' where he set up shop (drug dealing) in another city. Nas talked about 'One Love' with a lyrical letter from jail and later described the power of a gun from the first person of the gun. Tupac wrote a 'Dear Mama' letter that I could have shared word for word with my mom and talked about wanting to be a 'Soldier.' BIG gave me the '10 Crack Commandments' and talked about 'The Sky is the Limit.' And when Jay Z detailed 'D Evils' of the lifestyle of a hustler and explained how the 'Streets Are Watching', I had a soundtrack to hustle to.

I wanted to hear music that catered to my warped state of mind, I was a hustling, *dead president* chasing, *thug life* living, *American nightmare/gangster* hoping for a *good day* but also *ready to die.*

With growth comes change and while I still consider myself a lifetime member of Hip-hop, my current personal soundtrack leans more towards gospel music. I used to listen to Pac and Jay as I hustled and travelled the highways to have fun or do dirt (something illegal). Their music spoke to my life; it excited me and kept me ready for whatever may come.

I now get a new enthusiasm and inspiration listening to Kirk Franklin, Yolanda Adams, Donnie Mcclurkin, Tye Tribbet, Hezekiah Walker, Martha Munizzi and Mary Mary. It has nothing to do with the personal choices or lifestyles of the artists. There are many gospel artists whose personal lives are fouler than most Hip-hop artists. It boils down to what kind of music is resonating with your current walk in life. Is your personal soundtrack helping you and encouraging you to set a new example.

I will not give credibility to the notion that music can be blamed for a person's behavior. If someone commits murder and then blames it on the song he was listening to prior to committing the crime, we step into another level of the 'Don't Blame Me' mentality. We go from saying 'the *Devil* made me do it' to 'the *DJ* made me do it.' At the same time, we must also acknowledge the influence music has on our culture as well as our psyche. Jay Z said he wanted a crisp pair of jeans and a button up shirt and changed the dress code for Hip-hop overnight.

What I am saying is music, along with the other sensations we take in through one of our senses, can influence how we think. That is why I am so discouraged with the current state of Hip-hop. Not all of it, there are still some diamonds shining in the vast sea of mediocre mainstream madness. However, there is a vast shortage of genuine, real, soul stirring, goose bump providing Hip-hop.

We all have a personal soundtrack and that soundtrack can transition and evolve as we grow and mature, emotionally and spiritually. My challenge to you is to create a personal soundtrack that does not just speak to your current life, but inspires you to reach higher. Lauryn Hill said it best in her song '*Superstar*,' *Music is supposed to inspire.*

MISTI (Music Is Supposed To Inspire)

If we really are saying that rap is an art form, then we got to be more responsible for our lyrics. If you see everybody dying because of what you are saying, it don't matter that you didn't make them die, it just matters that you didn't save them.
—Tupac

Music is what feelings sound like.
—Author Unknown

I shared my love and experience in Hip-hop so that you would understand my forthcoming outrage. I see Hip-hop now as the prodigal son and I am waiting for him to come back home. I also feel obligated to 'holla' at some of these artists who are abusing the art. Please forgive my chastising tone, but this is a serious matter and some real talk is required. I will have to step on a few toes in order to get my point across. Consider it tough love. **Let's go to the streets!**

I have documented my drug dealing activities, none of which I am proud of, as well as my music business experience and I will admit there were a few times when the drugs and music crossed paths. I've dealt with producers who accepted marijuana as payment for tracks and studio time and I've met promoters who were not only engaged in bringing musical acts to their cities, but also had their hands in the drug trade.

I have also met independent artists who were financing their music dream with profits from their illegal drug dealing. I was one of them. I remember spending over $5000 to do a show in Atlanta that would pay me $1500. I didn't think twice about whether or not I was hustling backwards because I had the money and I wanted to do it.

With that said, let me emphatically state that these Hip-hop and R&B artists who have achieved a level of success that has propelled them to the top of America's pop culture, are not standing on corners selling drugs. No matter how many lyrics you hear them spit about still hitting the block and flipping 'birds' (kilos of cocaine), they are lying and if they're not lying, they're fools.

Let me talk to some of you 'rappers' for a second. Here it is, you have created a platinum recording and on it, you have songs talking about the drugs you are still selling and the gun you are still busting and all kinds of other criminal activities. You sold over a million copies! You are not still selling any drugs or trying to do anything that will remove you from your success. If you are engaging in these criminal acts and confessing them on an audio recording that can definitely be used against you in a court of law, well then you are crazy and I'm talking 'nuttier than a fruitcake' crazy.

There is no reason, whatsoever for a man to become successful and then glorify the struggle he has made it out of. You say you're keeping it real and representing the streets. Man, stop playing. Yeah, the streets are real and so was slavery. Are you going to represent that, too? Are you going to make songs about being the best cotton picker or how our 'hos' were sold away.

You can make the argument that we were forced into slavery so there is nothing to brag about, but are you then saying that because we **choose** to be thugs, gang bangers and drug dealers it makes it better? Is that sane?

The Civil Rights Movement was real, are you going to glorify that, make songs about how the dogs bit our people and how they took that water pressure from the fire hoses like OGs? If Malcolm and Martin had survived their assassinations, do you believe their future speeches would have boasted about the shots they took?

You are glorifying the part of the struggle we are trying to get our people to come away from. You make it cool to be a trapper, a hustler, a dough-boy. The truth is, you aren't on those corners. You aren't using your record deal advance to pick up a kilo and flip it three times. You aren't sticking up the dice game or anywhere else for that matter and you aren't going to bail out any of these young kids who allow your music to become their personal soundtrack.

Let us be realistic about keeping it real. You've seen some dark days; you had to do some ugly things because you believed your survival depended on it. You may have been shot, stabbed, abandoned by the people who are supposed to love you unconditionally. Somehow, you found a spark in your spirit that gave you the courage and strength to use a talent God gave you to go against the grain of what the 'hood' considers thorough. In turn, you wrote your own check out of the same pain and darkness that inspired every word you rapped or sung and every dream you had.

You won't ever be hungry again; your mom will never live in a project housing building or see roaches in her kitchen again.

Your children will never have to worry about what they are going to wear on school picture day. You've made it and you've done it the right way.

So how dare you make it out of the house that is on fire (the 'hood) and not go back to pull someone else out? Instead, you stand two blocks away with a megaphone yelling to those still inside to stay there, because it is beautiful there and that's where you're from and if they want to make it, just buy your album where you expound on the many ways to start their own fire so that they can have claim to their own flames.

How ignorant! Our people are in there dying or jumping out of the house and into prison. You stand there with a platinum chain around your neck that could have fed three families for a year talking about "I'm keeping it real." Real is reaching back to help some of those people who are still caught up in that struggle you're rapping about.

Imagine, for a second, your child leaves your house and as he or she walks down the street to the corner store one of your neighbors stops him and teaches him how to rob someone with a gun or a knife. Another neighbor calls from the second floor window and encourages your child to curse, to call women b&%*$ and hoes and to say f- you nigga, to anyone who doesn't like it. At the corner store, the cashier tells your child he/she will never amount to anything and that he/she should treat everyday as if it is their last; that they shouldn't care about anyone except themselves and to use any means necessary to get all they can.

Picture your child's little league coach teaching your son how to sell drugs or the cheerleading coach teaching your daughter how to strip dance. It's not a pretty picture is it? And if you're any type of parent you would not tolerate such negative and dangerous people around your child. So, this question is for those music artists and authors who glorify and promote the aforementioned activities; why, if you would not want your child encouraged in such a negative fashion, would you encourage mine?

You are not a role model, I know. I've heard it a thousand times; even from people who made a lot of sense when they said it. But ask yourself, are any of the people I mentioned above considered role models? Yet, they have access to our children. The difference is, your career, your livelihood depends on your influence on my child. We know the Hip-hop culture is not embraced simply because the music is hot. No, Hip Hop is adored because of its influence on popular culture.

Let me insert my disclaimer here before some of you who are really about the struggle take offense. I applaud you artists who provide a 'Street CNN' method to your music. If you are rapping about the state of the 'hood in an effort to document and shed light on what is really taking place and if your lyrics match the graphic images that many will never see unless they come there; I'm okay with that. If you want to be the reporter who brings the reality of the hood to the masses and if uncensored lyrical visuals become your high note that pierces the soul, well then, you keep doing what you do. Prayerfully, your words will spark the outrage that sparks change.

Music is supposed to inspire does not mean the music has to be happy or even positive. It means that it should motivate the listener to do something. Like change the way they think if their thinking is unhealthy.

Famous Doesn't Mean Focused

I'm focused man!
—'Best of Me' Jay Z

Even with everything I just mentioned, please do not assume I am calling on you to be a role model simply because you are in the spotlight. Not at all. I am calling on you to set a new example. I have made it clear that particular 'call out' is for everyone who holds this book in his or her hands and has ears to hear.

We can agree that being a celebrity has its privileges. The argument arises when we ask whether being a celebrity has responsibilities as well. I say yes, but I add it is the same responsibility of every God fearing human being. That is to love God, love your neighbor and love yourself.

This world, especially this nation tends to idolize a person based on their success. Should we follow an athlete, artist, author or actor simply because they have made a lot of money or entertained millions of people? Being famous is not the same as being focused. You become an example worth following by being focused in spite of being famous.

Many of these rappers/artists and athletes are the same children who grew up in the hood without authentic love and true guidance. They are members of a hurt generation and we see their pain in their art or worse in their publicized personal lives. If you weren't raised as a good person it is more difficult for you to bring it to your art.

These famous but not focused artists, athletes, actors, and authors are arrested and convicted for assault, robbery, drugs, guns and murder. They struggle with alcoholism and addiction.

They get in trouble for beating their wives and girlfriends and for sexual offenses that sometimes involve minors. They are caught driving under the influence; athletes get busted using steroids and performance enhancers to cheat for victory; music artists possess illegal drugs and carry concealed weapons illegally. Being famous does not mean being focused.

It is essential that we stop giving a separate set of rules to our celebrities, especially in their younger years when they are developing their character. Many of them get away with so much during their early rise to success; it becomes more and more difficult for them to understand that negative choices result in negative consequences. Thus, when they do something that necessitates more than a slap on the wrist or us looking the other way or, they fall very hard from a high place and struggle to get back up (get right).

Let me say this to you 'Superstars,' who believe you are bigger than life and even worse, above the law. I simply ask you to look at the history. You can break world records, win Grammys and Oscars and world championships; you can spend weeks, months or years on the best seller's list or Billboard charts; you may have millions of fans who cry and pass out when they see you, but make no mistake about it if you cross the line you will eventually be held accountable.

Be encouraged with this. You are blessed with a gift. That gift, your skill or talent, has allowed you to live a life most people envy. I don't have to tell you the fallacy of success being equal to happiness. Everywhere you go, there you are. If you aren't happy within yourself, if you don't have that self-love we talked about earlier you will not be a SANE person. You will simply have more things in your personal prison.

Many of you have suffered throughout your journey to the top. You have scars from your past and wounds that still need cleaned out. Your pain runs deeper than most because your success has given you the additional pressure of having to be everything to so many people; you lose the real you in the process of being an idol.

The shining light is in your ability to access the healing that fosters change. You have the money and time to invest in your inner well-being. Use it. There is nothing wrong with seeing someone who can help you deal with the pressure of fame or the unresolved pain from your past or present. There is no shame in being involved with programs that keep you grounded to the realities of everyday life so that your thinking isn't skewed by the adoration you receive from your public. Get the information and education you require and deserve so that you can truly live up to your potential to be an example worth following and supporting.

You must not be afraid to grow as an artist and as a human being. Tupac compared himself to a rose that grew from the concrete. You are that rose as well and I am asking you to stop bragging about how scarred your petals are and how strong your stem had to be to hold up in such a rough environment. No! Look at the fact that you grew from a form of matter not suitable for producing life. Brag about your growth.

Do not abuse your gift. The key to becoming a legend is humility. If you are humble enough to know that you don't know all the answers and humble enough to give and receive HELP you become eligible to say; "I'm focused, man."

Keeping it Reality

**Either you deal with what is the reality, or you can be
sure that the reality is going to deal with you.
—Alex Haley**

For those of us who are not superstars, we too, often focus on
the wrong things. One of the most frustrating objectives has to
be the desire to 'keep it real.' There is such fakeness to keeping it
real. Whose reality is real? It is time to start 'keeping it reality.'

We have athletes and entertainers who imitate the street
individuals in attempt to keep it real. The everyday people,
especially our young people, imitate the athletes and entertainers.
Then the 'unfocused' street individuals imitate the athletes and
entertainers, which means they copy a watered down version of
themselves. The cycle repeats itself and becomes worse every
time. If the street individuals present a better image, a new
example, the rest will follow suit and we would have a better
reality.

You have athletes and entertainers who refuse to leave the hood
in the name of keeping it real. I'm fine with that. If your success
and street credibility allow you to stay in the neighborhood you
grew up in without fear of being victimized by those who are
hungry and willing to do whatever it takes to eat, that's all good.
But don't stay there and not give anything back to the community
that raised you up. And don't be one of those artists who leave
the hood but keep the hood mentality with you.

Artists and athletes are making songs, commercials and
movies that make millions of dollars by exploiting what they see
the street individuals do. They throw it back in their faces, get

paid off it and don't do anything to help change the conditions. That is not keeping it reality. Many of them spend money on cars and jewelry and foolishness instead of giving back to the communities that supported them. That is not keeping it reality. From now on we need to put them on 'Front Street' in regards to their claims of keeping it real.

When you have the opportunity to ask one of these superstars a few questions make sure you ask them what they are doing to give back. I don't care if it's right after the Super bowl or a brilliant concert performance. If I'm doing the interview, I'm going to say: "Congratulations. Great job doing what you do. And before I forget, please tell the world how you are giving back to your community."

I extend those sentiments to you authors as well, especially those of you in the Urban Literature/Street Lit genre. You may not have the financial success and facial recognition of your athlete/entertainer counterparts, but you do have the same obligation to keep it reality. I have personal convictions in regards to the responsibility of the storyteller and his/her affect on society. I will hold my tongue until an appropriate time. I *will* say it is a blessing to see so many young blacks reading, especially young black males, but I'm not proud of the dissemination of street books filled with nonsense and glorified foolishness.

I recognize that some books are written strictly for entertainment and that is fine. Some books are meant to be eaten as meat (sustenance) and some are strictly feel-good junk food. But never should the junk food provide a true sugar rush that encourages the reader to do something heinous and unlawful.

You, as an author, are responsible for making sure you represent the words you write are fictional entertainment. Do not attempt to merge your real life with your art or encourage your reader to live out what you wrote. As I told the rappers, please don't glorify what you survived. Furthermore, take the time to study the craft of writing. I respect that you have an amazing story to tell and some money to help you get it out there. But that doesn't give you the right to put out a poorly produced paperback with very few paragraphs and even less punctuation. It is hard to teach a young person correct English so they can pass in school or pass the GED test when the books they are reading are grammatically incorrect. That isn't keeping it reality.

Authors, you must also reach back to your communities. You can donate books to schools and libraries and give writing workshops for youth centers and in prisons. You can do book signings at barbershops and hair salons and other businesses in the community so that our young people have the opportunity to see a real author in person.

I can tell you from experience; it is a beautiful feeling to have a child see me at a book event. I see their eyes light up as they realize that they too can become an author like me. That is the essence of setting a new example. That is keeping it reality.

We must address the images we are presenting to the world. We used to complain about the media perpetuating negative images. Nowadays, we eagerly offer those images and embrace TV shows that exploit them. We as a nation should be embarrassed by the way we are viewed by other nations.

Sure, you can say we are still the greatest country in the world and everyone and their mother wants to live here, but there is a moral breakdown in this country and we are a nation thirsty for spotlights. We will create a YouTube video of someone fighting, falling, or doing something sexual before we would post a video of someone picking their kids up from school or teaching someone how to read, write, cook or be a good role model.

Most of the reality shows today are premised on some type of awkward or degrading humiliation. These shows are scripted spectacles that are far from reality and create overnight celebrities. They also give a license to act foolishly. It is encouraged by the mainstream because it continues the cycle of degradation and provides a bad example. All in the name of high ratings.

The humiliation aspect is a part of the negative reason why reality shows are so popular. People enjoy being able to see others whose lives are worse than their own. They also enjoy the humorous situations where real people do real things. They get to see someone on TV do what they believe they would do in that certain situation all for the sake of 'keeping it real.'

I will admit that some of the reality shows provide a supportive view into lives that are similar to our own. Some of the shows provide the same 'breakthrough' reactions as 'group treatment.' We witness realities we believed were ours alone. We see other people struggling with the same issues. I will never forget the influence an episode of Keyshia Cole's *The Way It Is,* had on me and my treatment process.

It was the episode where she went to visit her mother in prison. Seeing them deal with the unresolved pain of her mother's addiction and neglect resonated with me, but it was the small detail of her mother, like my mother, losing her teeth that contributed to my breakthrough in being able to self disclose some of the pain I felt regarding me and my mother's relationship.

Some reality shows also provide a positive example of what can be accomplished through the arts. I am amazed by how many young people want to be dancers, singers, models and designers after watching regular people accomplish their dream of becoming a star on national television. The arts are a sure way of keeping our young people out of trouble. Some of the good reality shows encourage our children to strive for excellence in their respective art forms because they see firsthand what is required and what can be gained.

Reality is defined as 'the state of things as they actually exist.' When we keep it reality, we fall back on the honesty attitude and use the eye of a ref. We call it as we see it. We represent what is true and we live it and give it with no cut or sugar added.

'Keep it real' usually refers to some false image or a certain group's perception of what is real/true for them. We have to get pass the false images and the masks we wear to hide our true selves. We must not be afraid to be ourselves, to be what God has called us to be.

A good friend of mine recently told me that he believes I am the same person behind closed doors as I am in the public arena. He said that he is proud to say he knows someone who does what he says he is going to do, consistently. I am humbled by that compliment. I simply strive to keep it reality and set a new example. You should do the same.

If Not You... Who?

The greatest discovery of all time is that a person can change his future by merely changing his attitude.
—Oprah Winfrey

If you want more, you have to require more from yourself.
—Dr. Phil

You may not be a reality TV star, rapper, singer, actor, author, or athlete, but that does not give you 'role model' immunity. You are still required to set a new example, especially to the younger generation. To you men, you may not have given birth to this child you notice doesn't have a father or male figurehead in his life, but that doesn't excuse you from being a mentor or role model in his life. If you were raised properly, if you know the difference between right and wrong, if you have something positive to share, then you need to do that.

When you notice young men in your community who are on the wrong path, it is your duty to step in and set an example for them. I am not suggesting you take on the role of father; I am encouraging you to be a big brother, to be a mentor. That is something you are obligated to do. I'm not talking about simply taking the young kid out for ice cream, that's not mentoring. Mentoring is teaching him how to do something that will be productive in his life. Teach him things that will be an asset to his manhood.

I had mentors who taught me real estate and the stock market; men who taught me about eastern philosophies and politics; men who broke religion down to me. These were my mentors, but I didn't meet them until I was 22, 23 years old and already spending time in prison. That is why it is important for you to catch these young men while they're young and teach them these things before someone snatches them up and teaches them how to hold a gun or how to watch out for the police while the drug-dealers make their money and stay secure on the block.

It is crucial that you step out and grab hold of these young men. The same admonishment I gave to the rappers applies to you as well. These children are the future. Play your part in helping them make the future bright. For that matter, play your part so that the young man can be a part of the future. You have to step in and be a positive influence in his life. Set a new example for him to see and follow.

You women have the same responsibility. Some of you have been to college; you have overcome abuse, you have survived the rough years. You have made careers and become great mothers. You see this young girl in your community growing up super fast; she's already hooked on videos and believes her young body is her ticket out of the misery she calls home, and if not out, at least a materialistic boost from boys and men willing to pay for her time and attention.

You have to step in, and I'm not talking about teaching an etiquette class on how to hold a knife or fork for salads or sip tea with your pinky finger up. No! You have to talk to them about protection and why it would be beneficial for them to practice abstinence. Teach them how important education is and how much they can accomplish by finishing school and going to college. Talk to them about respecting themselves and why they should treat their body as a temple and a gift that should be saved for the person they will want to share that first submission and the rest of their lives with.

Women are nurturers by nature and that is why you make great mothers even at an early age, but early-age motherhood should be discouraged; especially by those of you who have experienced it. There has to be an early discussion of how to be a mature young lady without being sexually active. We have to teach young woman about being abstinent and how difficult it is to progress when you are trying to raise a child with no man at your side. Explain to them the struggle of being a single parent and how the child ends up being raised by the grandmother or a mix of the computer and television. All the while, the streets are whispering *'your daddy is out here.'*

It is your responsibility! Yeah, I will put it out there just like that. You, yes you reading these words right now, you are responsible for the young persons that you know need a mentor, big brother or sister. You are responsible for setting a new example. You are duty bound to step into these young peoples' lives. If you don't want your child/young loved one to be influenced by or taking under the wing of a negative person then you best make sure there are less negative people in this world for them to be influenced by.

SANE Challenges

1. Create a personal soundtrack. Find songs that speak to you and your situations and put them on your mp3, CD, iPod and/ or profile player. Share your personal soundtrack choices with loved ones who may benefit from hearing the song that gets you through when you are feeling down or the song that keeps you moving at the gym. And parents, pay attention to your child's personal soundtrack, communicate with them about what type of music speaks to them and you will be surprised how much easier it will be to relate to your child. Like the African villagers, you will know what song to use when they go off course of their path.

2. Join Big Brothers Big Sisters of America, or some type of mentoring program. Create your own program. Do whatever it takes to provide positive guidance in the life of a young person. Become a role model and set a new example for somebody.

PART 7

FAMILY VALUES

You don't choose your family. They are God's gift to you, as you are to them.
—Desmond Tutu

Taking the 'Diss' Out of Dysfunction

Before I go any further, let me make this very plain. I love my family. I have been blessed with a real, down to earth and diverse clan who loves me. Therefore, when I say that my family is dysfunctional, I say it with love and with a smile that says I am proud of my family in spite of our nonstandard way of living. For me, there is no diss in admitting our dysfunction.

I have one of those families who will go to war for one another with no questions asked. We may not be speaking to each other and we may not be allowed to step foot in one another's house, but if one of us is being threatened best believe the entire family will be there ready for whatever.

I remember the time my younger brother's father hit my mother. He had hit her before, but this time my brother and I felt we were old enough to defend her. We jumped on him and some of his friends jumped on us. We called our cousins and they came ready. My brother's father called his brothers, who drove to Harrisburg, Pennsylvania from New York City (a three-hour plus drive) in what seemed like less than two hours. They came six-deep and ready as well. They were from a dysfunctional family too.

We tore it up on Walnut St. One of those chaotic melees you see at high school sporting events. Men, women and children; throwing punches and wrestling on top of cars. It lasted about eight minutes. One of my aunts threatened to start shooting and the fighting grinded to a halt. When it was over, both families sat around drinking beer, laughing and complimenting each other on the good licks we got in. Dysfunction at its finest. Would you not agree?

I share that only to give the unfamiliar a glimpse into the unity and loyalty of a dysfunctional family and why we often become enablers to those family members who aren't sane. Why we rally for one another even when we are wrong.

I also want to shed light on why the family unit is so important in our mission to revive the village. The village is one large family. We must pay attention to the influence family has on each other. In the 'Impact of Victim Impact' section, I shared with you a mock letter from a younger cousin who was heavily influenced by me. Needless to say, I was influenced by older cousins as well; just as younger brothers and sisters are influenced by their older siblings and children are influenced by their parents.

In most families, there is usually a mix of positive and negative influence, but in dysfunctional families that mix is either very hot or very cold. I have two cousins (the ones I called first for the Walnut Street showdown) who were very close to me growing up. They were older than me by a few years and I idolized them, especially my oldest cousin. They were cool, great athletes, good dressers and man, they could fight. We were all growing up without fathers. We were trying to find our way into manhood without breaking our mothers' hearts or becoming victims to the streets.

These two cousins had their own personal prisons so what I am sharing now is not a diss, simply part of the dysfunction. My cousins would give us hand-me-down clothes and sneakers. Most of these things were better than what we could ever buy in a store. In their adolescent immaturity, they would sometimes tease us about having on their old things in the presence of their friends. Of course, if their friends said anything to diss me or my brother, my cousins would fight them right then and there.

These cousins taught me how to build Go-carts and fix bikes; how to hook up stereo systems and pick out colognes; how to talk to girls and where to get condoms. They also taught me how to get beer and steal cars, how to fake the punch and go in for the jack (body slam) and how to bag up a pound of marijuana into all dime bags. My oldest cousin would help usher me into the drug game, yet he also helped me buy my first house. Not a diss, just part of the dysfunction. His brother would make me fight other kids in the neighborhood as often as he could; he also made sure I was on baseball and football teams with him and that I always had a ride to practices and games.

These two cousins would have to tell you their own story as to who influenced them, but what I want to make clear is that even in our dysfunctional clan we had a love and loyalty that is rare in even your most functional families. These two cousins would pull guns out and plan to use them if you tried to harm me. There were plenty of times when I stayed at home pacing after being in a dispute, fight, shoot out; waiting for one of them to call me and tell me everything was fine; that I could go out with no need to look over my shoulder the whole night. Again, not a diss just some of the dysfunction.

I have an aunt who is only a few years older than we are. I smoked my first joint with her when I was 12 years old. Yet, she would also be the one to help me get my first car. I messed her credit up for years by defaulting on a loan she cosigned. I was also called to her house countless times to fight a boyfriend who had made the mistake of putting his hands on her. The sad part is me, my brother or my cousins would later in the month have dinner with this aunt and that same boyfriend we had beat up or at least escorted out of the house a few weeks earlier. Just a little more of the dysfunction.

I have another Aunt who practically raised me alongside my mother. This beautiful woman was always a safety net when things were bad at home. We usually lived in one of the houses she owned. She taught me how to dress and to be clean and to be proud of who I am no matter what I have. She taught me the value of money and the importance of saving. She bailed me out of prison at least three times. She also called the police on me when I refused to stop selling drugs in front of her house. As I said, this is definitely not a diss, I am simply providing details of the dysfunction that carries good and bad.

In a dysfunctional family, there is what I call the 'Bail over Business' mentality. In a dysfunctional family, you can be arrested for something you definitely did wrong and your family will be outraged about the injustice of it all. They will call around and have little meetings about who has what to put up and what Bail Bondsman is still willing to work with the family (dysfunctional families know a few bail bondsmen).

The family will come to the police station or preliminary hearing as packed as possible (dysfunctional families usually have a few members with open warrants who can't attend), and they will not leave until getting their family member out of jail. I have seen my family put up houses, cars, jewelry, TVs, and money to make sure I or another family member could come home.

Yet, if a member of the dysfunctional family wants to start a legitimate business, there will be very few supporters among their clan. This part is hard for me because I have a good family who loves hard. But I am being honest, we have definitely struggled with the 'bail over business' mentality. My family would rob Peter and not pay Paul to bail one of us out of prison. However, if a family member wants to open up a business or manage property, he or she will be hard pressed to get investors or start up money. The support will be there eventually, but a dysfunctional family has a hard time investing money into dreams. No, the money needs to be available for the inevitable nightmares.

This mentality has a lot to do with our conditions. We have been subjected to so much deprivation, need and disappointment that we keep a defensive mindset. We expect something bad to happen and we focus on being prepared to react. We react to what happens and do whatever it takes to survive in tact.

Bailing a family member out of prison is defense. Starting a business is offense. If we haven't played on the offense or been taught the offensive plays or schemes, then we are going to continue to play defense and defense only. Well, I am calling on, not only my family, but families all over this country; if we are going to set a new example; if we are going to revive the village we must learn to be on offense.

Trust me; it is bigger than 'bail or business.' Once we have families who have already mastered defense, learn to play offense too; we will have families that no longer require bail; families that own businesses they pass down through the generations.

As an offensive family, we have to start having family reunions planned out years in advance. We can't continue as dysfunctional families who see everyone together at the same time only at funerals. We must gather as often as possible, support each other's goals, and celebrate accomplishments.

My wife has a big family who has some dysfunction as well, but they have been practicing offense for some time now. We have travelled hours, at a moment's notice, to support family members being honored at church, playing in a basketball game or getting married. This is natural to my wife's family, because they have been doing it since they were children. To me, it almost seems competitive, but in a healthy way. Who was the only one not at Uncle So and So's cookout? Which cousin didn't make it to Aunt What's Her Name's wedding?

Speaking of weddings, as an offensive family we must abort this cycle of not getting married. We can't continue to set the example of being together with a partner and living together having child after child yet never dignifying that union with a God ordained ceremony or even a trip to the courthouse to make the union official.

Before I got married, I had been to one wedding my whole life. It was my aunt Marva, who had fed my siblings and me often and sent me the most amusing and inspirational cards while I was in prison. Her wedding was held in her backyard and was very beautiful, but I was already a 19-year-old 'playa' and I had gotten too drunk to remember the significance of what was going on.

I know for me, the lack of being exposed to married couples and witnessing the vow exchange of two people who enjoy a sincere and committed love affected the way I viewed relationships. I chose to be a womanizer. I am 'self accountable no excuses,' but I believe that as we become families on offense we must present a counter punch to the negative image of being boyfriend and girlfriend for over ten years with two and three kids born out of wedlock with different last names and no sense of what a family unit is based upon. It is time to turn 'baby mamas' into wives and 'baby daddies' into husbands. It is time to get on offense and set a new example. Let us go to the dinner table and talk about families on offense. Let us begin with the man.

Like Father Like Son

Like I needed my father, but he needed a needle.
—'My Life' by Game

Growing up can be a pain, you're not a man
until you come of age.
—'Boys to Men' by New Edition

The Letter felt hot in my hands. My father's handwriting, surprisingly similar to my own, scared and excited me at the same time. I hadn't seen nor spoken to him in over five years and our relationship had deteriorated long before that. My prison cell felt even smaller than usual. I gazed past the institutional gray locker and through the barred window with mixed emotions. I laid back on my bunk and reread the one page letter. I focused on the very last sentence: "I'll be there to visit you this Saturday."

It's interesting, the childhood memories we choose to hold on to. I can't remember my fifth birthday or the fire that destroyed my family's house when I was seven years old. But I can recall almost every detail of a visit with my father at the Dauphin County Prison when I was four years old.

It was summertime and the visitors' waiting lobby was stiflingly hot. My brother and I were almost a year apart, yet my younger brother was just as tall as me. My mother dressed us in khaki shorts and similar striped T-shirts. More than one person asked if we were twins. My mother wore sandals, faded jeans and a light-colored blouse. She had her natural afro picked out neatly and looked beautiful.

After what seemed like a ten-hour wait, (it was actually 20 minutes, but my 4-year-old attention span remembers it as much longer) we were led to a brightly lit room filled with fold out chairs and round tables. My brother and I sat side-by-side with our hands folded in our laps, swinging our legs nervously.

My father strolled in with a huge smile on his face. The first thing I noticed was how big he was. My father stood about six-feet, four-inches tall and had a lean muscular build. To me he was a giant. He hugged my mother tightly, and then kissed her on the forehead, nose, and lips.

"Look at my boys!" his deep voice sang out as he turned his attention to us.

He scooped us up into his arms at the same time and we squealed with delight at being so high in the air. His beard tickled my face and his kinky hair smelled like coconut. I also smelled spice cologne and a fresh soapy scent. My dad smelled very clean.

He walked us to the outside patio area and sat us atop of a scarred red picnic table. I squinted my eyes in the bright sun and noticed for the first time how dark my father was.

My mother is very light-skinned. She has a buttery complexion and my brother and I are only a shade darker. My father was swarthy. He had skin the color of tree bark or rich chocolate.

He kneeled in front of us and I remember holding his face in my tiny hands. His jaw was strong and he had deep dark eyes. He held my face in return and one of his hands covered my entire face. My brother grabbed our father's other hand and placed it on his face. This made my dad laugh and it was a sound so carefree, that it was contagious and we all laughed with him.

The rest of the visit was uneventful. My brother and I ate snacks while my mom and dad smoked cigarettes, held hands and talked.

Since then, I've seen my father sporadically and very few of those occasions hold pleasant memories. I've seen my father too drunk to stand up and too high to sit down. I've seen him lie, steal, and cheat as well as abuse women. I've seen him fight and win as well as fight and lose. He was like a shadow, tiptoeing in and out of my life trying not to cut his foot on his broken promises. I hated him and loved him at the same time.

My 12-year-old son could talk about broken promises, too. Although our bond is a lot stronger than what my father and I ever shared, he's still growing up without his father as an everyday presence. On our visits, his eyes light up and he smiles at me like I'm a clean-smelling giant or today's equivalent. But I wonder, if when he's back home, if I become a shadow to him as my father was to me; hovering on the periphery of his life.

On a recent visit, I told my son about a dream I had in which he told me he wanted to sell drugs like I did.

"You're crazy, Dad," he said with an uncomfortable smile.

"Oh, I'm crazy now?" I asked, pretending to be offended. "I wasn't much older than you when I chose the street life over everything else. I don't want you to ever make the same bad choices."

My son shifted in his seat, but held my gaze. "Nah!" he replied, shaking his head for emphasis. "Maybe if mom wasn't there for me I'd think about stuff like that, but she stays on me."

"That's good," I said with a knowing smile. "But what about all of the people who see you and talk about how much you look like me? Does that make you feel like you should be like me?"

"You said you want me to be better than you," he answered.

"I do," I replied.

"They just talk about your music and how I sound like you when I rap. And how I—"

"Can't dance, just like I couldn't," I interrupted and we laughed.

He paused for a few seconds, then said, "Sometimes, they'll say, 'you're going to be a gangster just like your dad.'"

"Do you think I'm a gangster?"

"No, you just got caught up in the system."

"That's not it, son," I said seriously. "I'm not in here because of the system. I'm in here because I tried to take a shortcut instead of working hard. It's nobody's fault but my own. I'm sorry for the time I'm missing in your life. All I can ask is for you to trust me and believe in me. I will never again do something so selfish to take me out of your life."

"You better not," he said while standing behind me with his arms draped around my neck; his way of giving me a hug and still be cool.

My father came to see me that Saturday as promised. He looked a lot older than when I'd seen him last, but he also looked better. He had lost weight and now looked more wiry than lean. He was clean-shaven and his salt-and-pepper hair was Caesar-cropped low. His eyes, were not as piercing as before, but still sparkled when he smiled. His mahogany skin had a healthy sheen.

He wore a fleece, FUBU warm-up suit and a pair of Nike sneakers. He looked like an old guy determined to get into a Hip Hop night club. When I said that to him, he laughed that same 'Kee-kee-kee-kee-keeee' that forces you to laugh with him.

We sat down. Father and son. And just talked. Religion, sports, politics, fatherhood, and anything else we could think of. The time flew by and when the end of visiting hours was announced, neither one of us wanted to move. As we stood to say goodbye, he asked me if I could ever forgive him. I nodded yes, knowing that if I didn't forgive him I would have to learn to hate myself. The black male as an absentee father has become a vicious cycle, but it can be broken, especially when we recognize the pattern and hold each other and ourselves accountable.

My father pulled me into a tight hug and whispered in my ear, "Just be better than me!"

I couldn't help but notice how clean he smelled.

I wrote that essay in 2003. My father would die from AIDS two years later. I would be released from prison two years after his death and my son would come to live with my wife and me two months after my release. I would love to tell you that because of my insight, I was able to come home and be the perfect father. And I would love to say that my son held true to his promise to bypass the streets on his way to becoming a man. But if I told you those things I would be lying.

Out of respect for my son's privacy, I won't go into the details about how we fought over whether I was supposed to be a father, friend or warden, but I will say that through it all we gained a deeper respect for one another. My son graduated from high school with a 3.25 GPA and received academic and athletic scholarships to a 4-year university. I give him all the credit for those accomplishments and I pray that someday he too, will write a book about the struggles he had to overcome during my absence as well as during our instant and complicated reunion. Maybe he will join me in these schools across America to discuss what becoming a man is really about; especially to the younger generation expected to end the cycle.

What I will talk about is the guilt that many of us men suffer from when it comes to our children and how we must do a better job of not allowing that guilt to affect our parenting. The guilt can come in many forms. My guilt was based on my absence as a father and I am sure many of you men have that same guilt even if you have never been to prison.

There are men who were absent in their children's lives even though they were living together in the same house. Some of you have a guilt based on physical and mental abuse. Abuse to yourself and to those you are responsible for. You're guilt may stem from the fact you were too hard on your child and you continued to punish them even when you realized their negative behavior was a desperate cry for attention and love. You handed out beatings when hugs would have been much more effective.

Many men have a deeply rooted guilt because they recognize they could be doing a much better job of being a father. We have to set a new example. Our young men are killing each other, their children and sometimes their parents. They are adopting gangs as their family. They are selling drugs and using drugs. They are dropping out of school. They are disrespecting and abusing women. Why? Because they saw us do it and they truly believe those are the things a man does to be considered a man.

It is sad because these boys want to be men so desperately; they go out and get a girl pregnant. They believe creating a child makes them a man. They are 15 and 16 year olds who have never learned to become men themselves, let alone teach someone else to be a man. They allow the babies to listen to the same profanity-filled music they enjoy and laugh when they hear their sons curse. They are destined to be man-children. They are lost and crazy.

I began this discourse on becoming an offensive family with a message to men because men are to be the head of the family. Too often, men are not even present in the home let alone prepared to lead their families. Come on brothers! If you have made it this far in the book, you have opened yourself up to being the man God has called you to be.

It is your time to shine. Our families are gifts to us and we must honor them with our love, respect, and support. We must correct them and set an example with our actions. If they follow our example, correction and discipline will not be needed as often. The family does not become a unit without you. The woman and children may still survive. They may even flourish and prosper, but when men no longer stand at the forefront of the family, the village as a whole is at risk of extinction.

Spirit Up

...but as for me and my house we will serve the Lord.
—Joshua 24: 15

Man up! That is what we say when we believe a male is not acting like a man. *Time to man up*. We say it to ourselves as an encouragement to face some type of difficult or arduous task. It has become a catchphrase to counter any display of softness or hesitation. Man up!

I have no problem with the positive motivation the 'Man up' command gives to those who are struggling with doing the things that manhood entails. Man up and get a job to help take care of your family. Man up and be a father to your children. Man up and take out the trash. Man up and marry the woman you have lived with and fathered children to. Man up and be a man.

I simply want to take it a step further and step into the higher realm of setting a good example. **Let's go back to church** for a second.

In Mathew 26:41 Jesus said to his disciples; *'Watch and pray, that ye enter not into temptation: the spirit indeed is willing, but the flesh is weak.'* And in Romans 8:4 it says: *'That the righteousness of the law might be fulfilled in us, who walk not after the flesh, but after the Spirit.'*

Instead of focusing on simply 'manning up', we must learn to 'Spirit Up.' You make excellent choices when your spirit guides you. Your spirit is your connection to God. When you make decisions based on the eternity of your soul rather than the temporary pleasure of your flesh, you will more than likely set an outstanding example. Spirit Up is the command for your spirit to lead you. If we are honest, we will admit that we make mistakes because we desire to please our flesh. The crimes we commit as well as the judgment errors we make in regards to our lives and the lives of our families stem from a failure to adhere to what our spirit says is righteous.

If you are so focused on providing a good home for your family that you are failing to provide a good father/husband for your family, you need to 'Spirit up.' If you are failing to cover your family and entire house with daily prayer, you need to 'Spirit Up.' If you fail to communicate with your loved ones how proud you are or how much you miss them when they are out of your presence and how much you love them, you need to 'Spirit Up.'

You must tap into the spirit of God that breathes within you. Use the love God has instilled in your very nature, through that spirit, as a motivator for how you speak and lead your family. You are a man with a Godly purpose and when your spirit leads you, you are an awesome instrument and tool of God. You will be used to help revive the village and change the world. If you do not believe you are ready, well then, you better 'Spirit Up.'

I wish I had the space in this book to recognize, commend and applaud all of the men who are setting a new example. My mission here is to draw more boys and men into that exclusive club of positive change by holding that mirror up for them to see the insanity they have adopted as normal. Nevertheless, I will take a moment to acknowledge that there are men who are doing the 'darn thing.' As I hold the mirror up to you, I am overjoyed to say that I respect your reflection.

To the men who are hardworking husbands and fathers, I salute you. To the men who married the woman they love despite the pressure to be a playa' or womanizer, I salute you. To the fathers who race their kids to baseball, football, basketball, volleyball, soccer and cheerleading practices; who try to attend every game, I salute you. To the young men who are going to school everyday, pulling good grades and preparing for college two years in advance, I salute you. To the young men attending secondary education as their family's first generation college representative, I salute you. To the middle school boys who focus on academics and athletics instead of stressing what the streets are calling for, I salute you.

To the men who have overcome drugs and alcohol addiction; who have survived prison; who have left the gang; who have turned away from the criminal lifestyle, I salute you. To the dad I saw last week carrying his sleeping daughter in one arm and holding his son's hand with the other as they crossed the street coming from church, I salute you. To the fathers I saw at the Boy Scout Pinewood Derby with model cars they worked on together with their sons or while their sons played video games and watched, I salute you and I will have more weight on my son's car next year, I promise. And to all of you men, big brothers, mentors, leaders who are making every effort to improve yourself, your family and your community, I salute you, I thank you and I pray for you daily as you continue to set a new example.

Girls Gone Wild

Courage allows the successful woman to fail-
and learn powerful lessons-from the failure-
so that in the end, she didn't fail at all.
—Maya Angelou

Let me talk with you ladies. It is a shame that after so many years of fighting to be treated with dignity and for the right to be heard and respected as equal voices in the world, many of you women and young ladies have embraced the negative, stereotyped-images of what a woman should represent. Many of you are not setting a good example.

You degrade yourself by dressing inappropriately, using foul language and sleeping around. Your fore parents fought for you not to be referred to as whores, hoes, B!*%$ and sluts or be treated like pieces of meat or second class citizens. You now embrace those derogatory terms. You wear them proudly. You post them on your MySpace and Facebook profiles. You address your friends with these offensive names and adopt the attitudes that go with the names. "Yeah, I'm a B, and I'm a good one, too."

Okay. I am not going to use this space to chastise you women who are in gangs and fighting teachers. I will not address the teachers who molest young students; the mothers who get involved with drugs and neglect their children or the wives who gave up on their marriage. I will forego my intentions to reprimand you women who drop out of school, get involved in stripping or prostitution, sleep around and fail to wait to have sex until marriage. I will not lecture those who have become criminals; who have lied, cheated, stole, assaulted and murdered and gone to prison.

We know there is a serious problem with women today and it has affected this nation as a whole, simply because the woman is and has always been the cornerstone of the American family. If the woman/mother isn't present, the family is handicapped. Throughout this book, I have made it clear how dismal the family situation has become. The breakdown of women is what causes me the most pain. I almost said fear, but I trust God and I know He hasn't given us the spirit of fear.

I have a wife, a mother, four aunts, two sisters and four daughters as well as a host of women in my life who I admire and respect. I would not be the man I am today if it weren't for the women in my life. Instead of elaborating on how 'wild girls have gone' I want to pull every single one of you into the arms of this book and hold you as God holds us in His loving arms. I want to tell you I understand and I believe in you enough to ask you to please look into that mirror and see what I see.

I See You

Psst! Excuse me miss. I'm not trying to embarrass you,
I was simply hoping you know how much I cherish you.
It's just…How can I put it?
Woman, you are amazing. And if I never said it or showed it,
I am so grateful and I'm saying thank you… right now.
Stand up lady and take a bow.
You are the who, what and how…
we become men.
I see you!

My attempt at eloquence feels incompetent.
What words do I choose for such an unwilling muse?
You smile with humility as you hear what I'm saying,
I praise your faithfulness and you say 'stop playing.'
You are the sustainer of life. Your womb is a planet
where life is planted and we take it for granted
as if it was us who planned it.
Such arrogance, such ignorance,
such indiscreet conceit
for us to celebrate that we grew
and not realize that we had to
if we wanted to catch up with you.
Shame on us for playing you; for treating love like a sport. We
came not only a day late and a dollar short,
but decades delayed and dead broke.
All we have is the hope… that you will forgive us… again.
That you will continue to give that unconditional love
that raises boys to men.
That you will turn from your mirror
after reaffirming the star you are
and take the time to look into our eyes
so deeply you see our fathers
when they were a boys.
And you can see the future, our future and
remind me who I am.
Because you know who you are.
I see you!
You are the woman, the queen, the mother, the wife.
You are the reason I know change is not only possible
it is mandatory, for without change

there is no happy ending for our story.

Without change, we will lose you.

And losing you is not an option.

I see you...

I dedicate those personal sentiments to all women. First, because I want you to know that only you can inspire that type of hope and love. Secondly, because I realize how difficult it is to be a woman today. I also see you crying yourself to sleep at night. You pray but the worry remains. I see you fighting to keep a smile on your face as you give and give of yourself, praying someone will say 'good job' or even better 'would you like some help.' I swear, I see you. You want someone to notice your pain. You have been there for people time and time again, but nobody is there when you need some HELP.

You don't want to compromise who you are, but you also don't want to be lonely or alone. You are aching inside your personal prison of apprehension. I see you! You are tired of being lied on and having rumors spread about you. You are sick of settling for any fool kind enough to say hi and ask you your name. I see you trying hard to be strong; to become the woman you are destined to be. I see you and I say to you, DO IT NOW!

You must be SANE (Self Accountable No Excuses) in regards to the areas of your life you need to address if you are going to set a new example. I also want to give you a little insight as to why even now you still have to be so much stronger than us men.

You have to let go of the thinking that has corrupted your morals and allowed you to accept less rather than demand more. Everything you are looking for can be found inside of you. You won't find it eating, working or shopping. You won't find it drinking, using drugs or having sex. Not even having a baby will fill the void you feel in your life. It is in your ability to love yourself and recognize who you can become.

You want to be a wife? Than you had better act like a wife even when you have no man. A man should look at you and see your spirit first. I don't care how beautiful you are, if you want a family, and I mean the real definition of family, you better look for the man who isn't staring at your chest or your butt. You had better find that man who is looking into your eyes in the same manner he looks into his mirror; you had better look for the man who can truly say, I see you.

If you want to be a part of this revived village; and truth be told I can't fake it and say *if*. You *have* to be a part of the revived village or there will be no village. You are the nurturing side of God's image; without you, we will have a fragmented and distorted view of the family paradigm.

We men are partly responsible for the state of emergency our women are in today. We learned at a very young age that women are to be viewed as objects; as less than men. Many of us learned that women are to serve us. Women, in turn, were taught that men have suffered more and are required to do more so should have a greater role.

This is the division that has destroyed the family. It is also untrue. Initially, we suffered the same. Later, women suffered at the hands of the men who believed their wife, mother, sister or girlfriend deserved to bear the brunt of all the frustration they couldn't express on the job to their boss or to their peers on the streets. Not to mention, the abuse and molestation you suffered while being reared in some *very* dysfunctional families.

It is a new day. And there is definitely a new example to follow. Woman you need to allow yourself the freedom to search beyond what you deem as comfortable. As hard as it may be, you must let go of the pain that keeps you a victim. You have the right to demand better than what you witnessed as a child. Just because men abused your mother doesn't mean you have to suffer the same mistreatment. That isn't love. And if your father wasn't present in your life, you can not make it a mission to look for a father in your boyfriend or husband.

Hold on one second and let me holler at the men again. Do you see what happens when we fail to be fathers? We aren't leaving only boys behind when we fail to accept our responsibility and we become addicts and/or go to prison. Desensitized daughters are left behind as well, and they grow up without fathers and look for love from boys too early in their young lives. They long for love so desperately; they turn to premature sex and become parents long before they become adults. They have no idea what the family dynamic consists of and they succumb to many of the aforementioned personal prisons. More and more frequently, they commit acts that lead to being locked up in a physical prison.

When a woman goes to prison, the family unit is broken. We mentioned earlier how women are currently the fastest grow-ing prison population. Think about what that does to the family structure. Even after their release, can you imagine how hard-ened they have become? These women go months and years without visits, without being able to hold their children, hug their parents, or express their emotional, nurturing nature. They are bitter and angry. They have to struggle to get back on their feet and often have to prove they are capable of taking care of their children.

Listen ladies, if you are doing anything that may lead to you going to prison I implore you to stop it right now. You have options, I promise you. You simply have to change your perception. Not all is loss. The whole world isn't against you. Love is not defined by how many gifts a man buys you or how hard or often he hits you. If you are ready to accept change in your life and to set a new example, the opportunity is staring at you from that mirror and all you have to do is open up your heart, spirit and mind and say "I am ready to feel the way I want to feel. I am ready to change!"

If you are truly ready, one of the first things you are going to have to do is cut some people off. Yeah, just like that. Cut them off. We all have some bad connections in our lives, but you women are the ones who struggle more with letting them go. There are people in your lives who are not good for you. You have to love them from long distance because you will not become a better example if you are still surrounded by bad examples.

It's sort of like being a fish. You leave the dirty pond you lived in all your life. You get all cleaned up (change). Your gills are clear and breathing in fresh air. But if you are thrown back into that dirty pond, pretty soon you will look just like the rest of the filthy, scum-filled fish that never left (changed).

Let me tell you about those dirty fish, those bad connections. You know how they say 'misery loves company' well one of my former pastors told me that misery loves *miserable* company. It isn't enough for you to be around them, you have to be miserable, too.

Bad connections are those 'so called' friends who are always finding a way to rain on your parade. Even if the parade hasn't started yet; you may have only set the date and they will forecast some rain for you. These 'friends' are always trying to get you to go somewhere you don't belong. They are bad connections. These are the friends who talk about you behind your back. They lie on you and spread rumors about you. If you have a man, they either hate him or want him or both. You have a job to go to in the morning and they want you to go to the club with them. You have homework to do and they want you to stay on the phone and talk about all the boys in school. They are bad connections. And they will hurt you just because they can.

You cannot continue keeping people in your life who aren't good for you. I understand the false feeling of needing to keep these bad connections. I made the same mistake. I didn't want to let go of all of my past so even though I gave up the drugs, I still hung around with people who smoked and drank. I wanted to feel as if I still belonged. I eventually learned to break away from those bad connections. You have to do the same. You have to be strong enough to walk away from the people who aren't SANE.

That includes the men you are involved with. If he's not right and he's not trying to get right, let him go. If he gets right, he'll be back and if he doesn't well then you have done yourself a favor and probably prevented a lot of drama and heartache. Can I keep it reality with you women? I just shared a poem with you that expressed how much I love and value you, so can I have a few minutes to talk heart to heart with you?

Let me tell you women something and this goes for whether you are 15 years old or 50 years old. I am all for the I-N-D-E-P-E-N-D-E-N-T woman who has her own and doesn't rely on a man to define or complete her. That is all well and good. But if you are going to be a wife, mother and matriarch; if you intend to have a family and still be a female who is focused, fabulous, inspired, blessed, proficient, professional, poised and motivated. You must first be virtuous. You must find that balance of being a partner who respects the headship of the man in your life while recognizing your role as Helpmate.

Don't start trippin' about the mention of headship. There is no secret that real men lead their families but real women run their house. Instead, focus on the mention of Helpmate, which is defined as 'a helpful companion.' Then look at the word virtuous, which is defined as 'being chaste and having or showing moral goodness or righteousness.' The Bible says this about the virtuous woman in Proverbs 31:

Who can find a virtuous woman? for her price is far above rubies. Verse 10

The heart of her husband doth safely trust in her, so that he shall have no need of spoil. Verse 11

She will do him good and not evil all the days of her life. Verse 12

She riseth also while it is yet night, and giveth meat to her household, and a portion to her maidens. Verse 15

She considereth a field, and buyeth it. Verse 16

She stretcheth out her hand to the poor; yea, she reacheth forth her hands to the needy. Verse 20

Her husband is known in the gates, when he sitteth among the elders of the land Verse 23

She openeth her mouth with wisdom; and in her tongue is the law of kindness. Verse 26

She looketh well to the ways of her household, and eateth not the bread of idleness Verse 27

Her children arise up, and call her blessed; her husband also, and he praiseth her. Verse 28

Many daughters have done virtuously, but thou excellest them all Verse 29

Favour is deceitful, and beauty is vain: but a woman that feareth the LORD, she shall be praised. Verse 30

Can I get an Amen! As a virtuous woman, you are rare, precious, trustworthy and kind. You are disciplined, good with money, compassionate and generous. You are influential, wise, distinguished and praiseworthy. Best of all, you are God-fearing and therefore you are honored. I could preach for days about the virtuous woman. You should be able to read those words and feel a stirring in your spirit that sets your heart, mind and body on a specific mission to be a righteous example for all women to follow.

Now get this, Queen. Here is the jewel I want you to grab and put into your crown. You too, are able to 'Spirit up.' I wouldn't dare tell a virtuous woman to man up, but I will encourage you with love to Spirit up!

You have to allow your spirit to lead your every decision. If you are stuck in a dead relationship where love is only a word used occasionally, you need to Spirit up. If you are sleeping around and using your body to gain the attention you yearn for, you need to Spirit up. If you have children who are looking to you as an example of what they can become, you had better Spirit up.

Over 5.3 million women are abused each year. An intimate partner kills 1,232 women each year. Domestic violence is the leading cause of injury to women. The Aids virus is the number one killer of women ages 25 to 34. Women are joining gangs, going to jail and dying from AIDS in record numbers. There is no denying the need for women to Spirit up.

When you pick a partner using your spiritual judgment, it is very unlikely you will pick a man who will abuse you. When you Spirit up, you consider the fact you are putting your life in someone else's hands every time you have sex and you make sure the man is worth you taking that risk.

As a virtuous woman who spirits up, you recognize that being a Helpmate implies partnership. And as a partner you must be equally invested in the future of your family. You should not have a problem encouraging your husband to pray and cover you and your family. If he isn't working you push him to get a job, if he dropped out of school, persuade him to get his GED. You must spirit up and demand that your man do the right thing, especially if he is involved in some harmful activities and his decisions can have a residual affect on you and/or your children.

I'll make it plain because I am a man who was guilty of this sick transgression. If you allow a man to bring drugs, guns, or gang activities into the home around you and your children then you are just as guilty as they are. What type of woman allows her life and the lives of her children to be put in jeopardy because she thinks she loves a man who doesn't care enough about her to protect her from his dangerous lifestyle?

Even when you are involved in a relationship or a marriage, you must take the time to look into your mirror and make sure you are giving and receiving not only HELP, but your undivided, absolute best. Do not settle for less than you deserve and do not deny your partner the best you have to give. Herein lies the success of a healthy relationship and begins the unbreakable bonds of a true family.

Reviving the Village

Children have never been very good at listening to their elders, but they have never failed to imitate them.
—James Baldwin

Once the man and woman come together as a strong, God-fearing family unit, it is now time to expand their mission and revive the village. It starts in the home with the immediate family. We must get ourselves on task and then bring our children into this new way of thinking.

Our children are crying out for correction. They want more supervision and discipline; they want to know their parents care about them enough to stop them from doing the wrong things. Parents are allowing their children to grow up by themselves. Sure they provide the necessities or spoil them with gifts, but they have no idea what their child is up to or in to. The kids do not have any respect for their parents. You wonder why a man disrespects his girlfriend or wife; he does it because he may have never learned to respect his own mother.

We cannot continue on the path of ignorance when it comes to what our children are learning outside of our homes. I was a little hard on the 'superstars' in the Role Model chapter, when in all truthfulness, the most influential people in our children's lives should be the parents. If parents are doing their job, it won't matter what stupidity they see or hear outside of the home. Teach the children right from wrong and equip them with the knowledge of choices and consequences, and in all likelihood, the children will make good decisions.

Once again, it goes back to communication. We as parents, must learn fruitful ways to communicate with our children. We have to be aware of our children's influences that are outside of our scope. There comes a time when our kids will look at us and not consider us as being cool. If we did our job correctly, even labeled as 'Not Cool' we will still be sought after for sound advice.

If we have paid attention to who our kids consider as friends and what type of music they are listening to; if we have been honest with them and treated them like young people and not our property, we have more than likely earned their trust. Communication should come naturally. However, the communication must be a dialogue, don't just give them a command to do what you tell them. Take the time to ask them for input on the things that involve them. Show them that you respect their opinion and allow them, with your guidance, to make certain decisions for themselves.

You can't just give your child toys to play with and a TV to watch and expect them to have a good rapport with you. You have to give them time, love, and a dependable environment. You must show them that you respect what they are going through and what they feel, so they can be more receptive to the advice you give them. You must be an Assertive parent, not a Passive (doormat) parent and not an Aggressive (dictator) parent.

Your kids are on social networks; MySpace, Facebook, Friendster and different Ning sites. They are being exposed to inappropriate people, pictures and language. Make sure you are aware of what they are doing and protect them by any means necessary. Even if it means being that unpopular parent who wants to see and know what their child is involved in.

We talked about the perils on the streets, and on the internet, but what about the schools. Many cities have schools with kindergartners and first graders going to school with eighth graders. My sister had to explain pads and menstrual cycles to her 7-year-old daughter, who saw an older girl who had an 'accident' in the bathroom at school. The children are becoming fluent at cursing and they are learning that being 'nasty;' is cool as they witness the hormonal relationships of the 'cool' teenagers they go to school with.

It is serious out there. Between the streets, school, computers, music and TV; you had better talk to your kids about peer pressure, drugs and sex. Ask them questions and be sure to listen to their answers. When I speak at different schools, I often hear from the students how they wish they could talk to their parents the way they just spoke with me during the question and answer session of my talk. Do you hear that parents? Your children want you to talk with them about the pressures and problems of being a kid, an adolescent, teen and young adult.

They want you to help them understand. They are the same kids who as little toddlers asked you why about everything. Your child is still curious and you must have empathy and remember there was a time when you were curious as well. You were also an imperfect child at one time. Don't you dare get all self righteous about your child getting into a fight or missing their curfew. Have you never done the same? Our children heard the stories about our past. Grandparents make sure of that. If we fail to communicate our experience along with our guidance, our children will rightfully view our discipline as hypocritical.

It is all about communication. As parents, you have to be aware of what your children are doing and as children, you must keep parents informed so there is an atmosphere of trust. For you young people who want to practice being assertive communicators, I challenge you to take the initiative to engage your parents in conversation about some of the things you would like to discuss with them.

Parents, it is your responsibility to assure your child that when you are checking their cell phones and computers for inappropriate texts, pictures or messages; that you are doing it to protect them not to invade their space. You can explain to them that you have the right to see what they are being exposed to and their 'privacy rights' become fully invoked when they are living in their own home and paying their own rent or mortgage.

Seriously, remind the children that there are humans behind those computers and you have more experience with the human dynamic. Tell them you want to keep them safe because you love them. I love it when I see a young person's MySpace page and one of their parents is their top friend. That tells me there is some healthy communicating going on.

Try to avoid being a dictator parent or a detective when it comes to checking on your child's internet activities. Do it right in front of them. Say something like, "let's take a look at your MySpace page." Then use that opportunity to reinforce when your child is doing the right thing. Let them know if their page truly represents who they are.

My 15-year-old daughter is involved in ROTC/AVID, cheer-leading, eating and being as silly as she can be. She isn't thinking about boys...yet. It doesn't surprise me that her MySpace page has a SpongeBob Square Pants background and she claims to be from Chickentopia. She is using a social network to express who she is and she has enough self-esteem not to care what anyone else says.

When you are doing your parenting thing right, you have a positive and open rapport with your children. One time, I asked her about one of her close friends who I hadn't heard her talk about in a while. She told me they weren't as close as they used to be. When I asked her why, she simply shrugged and said, "She went all high school on me." I didn't have to ask what that meant. She has learned from her mother and me the disadvantages of growing up too fast and has no problem 'cutting you off' if she believes that is what you expect from her.

Being a family that is SANE is so essential. We have to take into consideration that in this day and age there are many examples of the nuclear family. I know that many of you reading this book are single parents. Some of you are widowed or divorced. Some of you may have made past mistakes that blessed you with beautiful children and are now waiting patiently for your soul mate or husband. Some of you are raising children who aren't biologically yours. Some of you are in blended families. Some of you are single with no kids.

My point is you are still eligible and obligated to contribute to the revived village. You are a part of the village and even if you do not have an immediate family you are a member of the community family and you, too, have work to do. Turn back to the 'If Not You, Who' chapter if you need a reminder.

The Middle Generation

One generation shall praise thy works to
another, and shall declare thy mighty acts.
—Psalm 145:4

It takes a whole nation to help me
raise this generation
—'A Whole Nation' by Kirk Franklin

As we step out of the home and into the village, we identify three groups–Three Generations. There are always three main generations sharing this world at the same time. They are the young generation, the middle generation and the senior generation. If one of those three is missing, you no longer have a civilization. You will have unbalance and disorder. You also have a sense of chaos when the interconnectedness of these three generations does not exist. There is that lack of a connection today and it is the cause for the current confused and 'crazy' state of our nation.

There has been a cultural collapse of the village. The young generation has been ignored and rejected. The continuum of confusion is due to their dreams being dismissed or destroyed. We have failed to encourage and inspire the visions of our youth; they have in turn failed to live out the dreams of their childhood. We have learned the hard way that when the young generation doesn't have a dream to follow they become a nightmare.

The loss of unity is a result of the senior generation being disrespected and their experience, unappreciated. We have almost lost an inherent part of our future with our failure to seek the wisdom of those who have survived such a turbulent past. We as a community face many problems and we have disregarded the people who have answers based on experience.

It only takes for one of these to happen in order for the climate to change, but when both of them occur at the same time, which is the situation we find ourselves in today, it becomes a thunderstorm of disarray. It is almost impossible to be a cohesive, unified village if these two generations are foreign to each other.

It is our job as the middle generation to be a bridge for these other two generations. It is our role and our responsibility to keep the young generation and senior generation connected. We cannot continue to be the generation that advocates, condones or turns a blind eye to the rejection and disrespect of the other two generations.

You are a member of the middle generation from the time you become mature enough to set an example others should want to follow up until the time you can no longer function in your right mind. There are no technical age requirements. You may be 13 years old with younger siblings who look up to you or you could be 65 with a living mother and father you still admire. That is why the middle generation is so integral to the success of the village; they have the responsibility of connecting the youth and the seniors even when that means leading their peers.

The middle generation must lift up and recognize the work of the senior generation. We are obligated to keep the senior generation involved. We should treat them as the pillars of our present circumstance. Many of them are tired and they are justified in their belief they have done enough work that they should be able to relax and enjoy the twilight of their lives.

We have to remind them that their presence alone is an inspiration and encouragement to us to live a life that will allow us to reach the pinnacles they have attained. We must also make sure they are not afraid of the other two generations.

For the junior generation we serve as the parents, teachers and coaches. We are their immediate guides, protectors and correctors. We must link them to the senior generation so that they respect the foundation of our morals and values. They must respect that, while the middle generation are the ones who can be keep up with them physically, it is the senior generation who provides the wisdom and knowledge we share with them. We must let them sit at the feet of the seniors and hear first hand where the middle generation received its focus.

It is the role of the middle generation to make sure our youth are accepted. That we follow the command of Jesus who said suffer the children to come. We must eliminate the mindset that says, 'children should be seen and not heard.' We must let them know we respect their opinion and their dreams are what our futures are based on. There is no war between these generations only a lack of understanding. Not to beat a dead horse, but again, understanding comes from communicating.

The Senior Generation wants the younger generation to talk differently and pull their pants up. Well, my fellow middle generation and National Exhoodus Council member, Dr Divine Pryor spoke truth when he said; "if we pull their minds up they will automatically pull their pants up."

The Younger generation wants the senior generation to show them the same respect they demanded when they were younger. Well, then we must reinforce the position of giving respect to gain respect.

In order to set a new example we must toss out many of the old examples. The village has to get past our past misconceptions. The angst that exists today is bigger than the Baby Boomers versus Generation x or y. It isn't about conservative versus liberal or young versus old. The crisis we are facing today is based on the absence of love. We need love to rebuild the bridge that will reconnect the entire village.

A 90-year-old deacon, who is a pillar in the church, his family and his community, guides me. He has done enough work in his lifetime to say, "I'm going to just sit here and listen, okay?" He's not sure if he is still of any use to the church or the community. I explained to him how I count it a blessing every time I witness him stand up and speak or pray and how his presence alone brings humility to everyone else because we know we are in the presence of history.

Here is the connection that must be made. My eight-year-old son explained to this deacon how he knew Barack Obama would be elected president because they did a mock election at school and Obama won that, too. The deacon smiles and explains how he never believed he would see the day this country would elect an African American as president.

When my son asks why, the deacon gives my son some of the history that explains why the victory means so much to him. His words add to my son's pride. My son, in turn tells him how "all the white people like President Obama too, and won't act like they used to." His words add to the deacon's hope. Together, they present the new example of a revived village.

At the 2008 Harlem Book Fair, I was signing copies of my first book when a three-generation, mother, daughter and grandmother, came to my table. These three beautiful women were filled with love and excitement as they shared with me how much they loved reading. Like many families, the daughter was raised by the grandmother who introduced her to the world of books. The daughter, when reconnected to her mother, who had also inherited that love of words from the grandmother/mother, was able to forgive, rebuild and revive. Three generations, maintaining their connection and representing their family and their revived village.

We were in our monthly Men's Group meeting discussing the possibility of doing some things with the Boy Scouts. Our Secretary, who is also a Reverend and in his 40's, mentioned that he was never able to receive his Tenderfoot ranking as a scout because he never learned to tie a taut-line hitch knot or a square knot. We teased him a bit and then moved on to other business.

The following month, at our next meeting, after donuts and coffee were passed around and the prayer was said, our Men's club president (who is in his 80's) pulled out two ropes and showed the Reverend how to tie the two different knots. Once the Reverend tied it himself, our president reached into his folder, pulled out a handmade merit badge, and pinned it to the Reverend's shirt. Although we laughed and enjoyed the levity of the moment, I don't think it slipped pass any of us how much that kind act meant to the Reverend or to us witnessing it. He kept the badge on the whole morning and I wouldn't be surprised if he wore it the entire day.

I observed that good deed as a member of the junior generation and learned from a member of the senior generation who was giving HELP to a member of the middle generation. Do you see how we have the ability to interchange our role in the village depending on the situation and the other village members involved? There are times when I am with my oldest daughter and youngest daughter and I fall into the senior generation as my oldest represents the middle and helps me relate to what the youngest is dealing with.

In order for there to be a revival of the village, we have to rebuild our families and reinvent our communities into villages. Once we have the family unit on point we can expand from a cookout in the back yard to a block-party on our street to a community festival. We need to have days when the elderly generation just come out and sit on their porches and the middle generation takes the younger generation through the neighborhood and introduces them to the senior generation.

We must take our grade school children to visit the seniors who are in nursing homes and care centers. We must invite members of the senior generation to come speak in classrooms in the schools and share some living history with our kids. The middle generation has the biggest responsibility and that is to maintain the trust, love and respect of the three generations. It is our responsibility to change the current climate of our communities.

Climate Changer

I feel it in the atmosphere...
—The Presence of the Lord by Kurt Carr

I am a firm believer we cannot change anyone. We can point to the water; we can drink it in front of them and tell them how good it tastes, but if they don't want to drink we can't make them drink. However, by changing the example we set ourselves we give those who see us more options. Our family and friends who look up to us; see us and witness our actions and they receive another example to reflect on when it comes time for them to change their thinking. In order for us to set that new example, we must become climate changers.

There are people who walk into a room and instantly change the climate. They bring a new spirit into the environment and somehow manage to motivate all who are present. You can look at the historical leaders throughout history from Alexander the Great to Abraham Lincoln; from Gandhi to Dr King; from Oprah Winfrey to President Obama; all possess a remarkable ability to change the climate.

The charisma may be innate and the leadership may be inherent, but being a climate changer is also a learned behavior. You can do it, too. You have the ability to use your encouraging attitude and your new way of thinking to bring about that positive charge of lightning that brightens and electrifies the atmosphere. In order for us to revive the village, we must change the climate.

In order to be climate changers we must set a new example. We start by changing how we think, which changes how we behave and how we feel which changes how we are seen and received by others, which changes the climate and inspires our families as well as our communities. So, although, I do not believe we can change people, I know for sure we can definitely change the world.

SANE Challenges

1. Spend family time at least once every other week. Play games, watch movies, go camping, on a picnic or to the park. Have dinner together as often as you can and talk about what is going on in your lives.

2. Mentors, Big Brothers and Sisters take your young people to a wedding. Allow them to see what it truly means to have a loving and committed relationship that is established by two people standing before God, family and friends and vowing to love each other for better or for worse. Let them get dressed up and witness the beauty of marriage and a real wedding and in doing so, reinforce to them what they should dream of having someday.

3. Fathers, set Father-Son days with your boy(s). Use these times to really bond and open up the door for man-to-man communicating. Show your son(s) how to think and act outside of that box that attempts to define who they should be. For your daughters, do the same. Have little Daddy-Daughter dates, where you show your daughters healthy love and attention while providing them the example of the type of man they should one day seek.

4. Memorize the SANE Initiative (Pledge, Mission and Goal), and be able to recite it on command.

THE SANE INITIATIVE

The Pledge

This is my oath, this is my vow
I am ready, the time is now
The mission is Love, the goal is change
My mind is renewed, I am SANE!

The Mission

I am a positive role model
I can make choices that make a difference
I will be responsible, honest and kind

I am the potential of a promising future
I can set a new example every day
I will change this world; one mind at a time.

The Goal

Set A New Example.

I AM SANE!

And be not conformed to this world: but be ye
transformed by the renewing of your mind, that
ye may prove what is that good, and acceptable,
and perfect, will of God.
—Romans 12:2

I began this book by talking about my past insanity and asking; Are You SANE? I could have easily spent a lot of time and many pages discussing the sanity of this world we live in today. I quoted one of my favorite scriptures above to show you that the Bible tells us we are not to be conformed to this world. We are to be transformed by the renewing of our minds. Renew our minds. Transform, change our minds. We must have new minds.

I could have shared my thoughts and facts about the deplorable conditions of some school systems and communities, which are based upon years of government neglect, and have attributed to the downward spiral of its residents into drugs, gangs and crime. I could have talked about personal experiences with the disparity that exists in the criminal justice system and how certain unfair laws added to the reason why more minority men are going to prison than college.

I could have spoke on housing laws that prevent formerly incarcerated people from benefitting from subsidized housing and how the family structure is ruptured because the young father has a felony and the mother lives in public housing, which doesn't allow the convicted felon to live there. I could have addressed the systematic racism and sexism that still exists in colleges and corporations; or how in 2009 there are still hate crimes being committed across this country.

I wanted to talk about Health issues and HIV statistics; Re-Entry programs and voting rights; juvenile justice and child abuse. I wanted to talk about the violent, vicious, and volatile images that are perpetuated through the media and expound on how much of a negative impact it has had on the sensibilities of our minds. I want to talk about what is wrong with the world.

And I will. But this book here is my answer to someone asking me the question "What did you do?" In the same manner we ask someone to be accountable for when they've done something wrong, this book is my answerability for how I have been able to do something right. All of those things I mentioned are important and they are on my agenda. But I chose this book to counter the Enemy's most successful tactic against God's people–attacking their minds.

There are people who have been physically wounded and they still worship God. There are people who have been struck with all types of diseases and they still worship God. There are people who have lost their parents or children to early deaths and they still worship God. But when you have someone who the Devil has succeeded in attacking their mind; someone who has lost their mind? You have someone who doesn't know God, doesn't love themselves or anyone else and will commit themselves to a life of insanity.

This book is for those who need a new mind. Those who need to renew their mind. That is the awesomeness of God; that He can take someone like myself who was lost and not SANE and then use me to show his power and ability to transform and renew. I can't help but tell my story and know that it will be to God's credit and to His glory when a reader looks into that mirror and decides to change their life by changing their mind. So, this book is dedicated to the individual who wants to renew their mind–who wants to set a new example.

The Doors to the Church...

At the end of most church services there is an invitation that usually begins with the words; 'The doors to the church are now open.' This gives a person who has been convicted by something they have heard or seen, by way of the Holy Spirit, the opportunity to accept Jesus and the love of God and to transform their lives by renewing their minds.

While this book is not a sermon, I have testified, taught and preached a little. I shared with you how my ability to set a new example stems from a new way of thinking that revolves around a spiritual transformation that has given me the courage to step boldly into the open doors of the church and then become an open door to the church. I am a living testimony of how God's love, grace and mercy creates in us a new mind and a clean heart. It is only by God's divine will that I am SANE. God will do the same for you.

If you truly desire to be SANE, you must recognize that the doors to the church are open. You need to turn to the God who created you, who kept you, who protected you, who rescued you time and time again. You need to fall into the arms of the God who has allowed you to survive all of the bad decisions you have made throughout your life. Yes, the doors to the church are open and if you have never experienced true love you need to look no further than the love of God who sent His only Son to die so that we could live. Everything I have shared with you in this book is summed up with these words: I am SANE because I am Saved.

I will bring this part of our journey to a close and share with you this amazing revelation. I have worked on this book for over a year and it started as I said earlier, just to answer the question of how I went from crazy to SANE. However, as with most journeys something happened along the way. Here is the remarkable and startling culmination of my testimony and a preview of my next step in setting a new example.

On March 11, 2009, my job sent me to Washington DC to be an exhibitor at the US Law/GovSec Expo, which was being held at the Walter E Washington Convention Center. Around seven pm, I received a call from my friend Tony, who had just gotten off of work and was going to come pick me up so we could get a bite to eat. I figured I would take a walk while I waited for him and I headed down Seventh Street NW.

Somewhere around Seventh Street NW and I Street NW I was approached by a man who was a little bigger than me, dressed neatly and wearing a wedding band. I describe him only because it surprised me when he asked me in a real humbling tone if I could spare some money so that he could get something to eat.

His exact words were; "I hate to even ask you this, brother. It's not about the money, I just got out a few days ago and I'm struggling. I want to get something to eat and I was hoping you could feed me."

He had me when he said he 'just got out.' As a formerly incarcerated person, I could empathize with that statement. I gave him five dollars. He smiled, thanked me and said he was headed to McDonalds and its Dollar Menu. I don't know if he really went to McDonalds or if he used the money for food. Nor is that relevant to what I am sharing with you.

I ended up waiting over 90 minutes for Tony to pick me up. I walked down Seventh Street NW to the Verizon center where the Wizards were playing the Hornets. I was standing at the entrance of the Gallery Place Chinatown Metro Station as the game was letting out.

I stood there and watched the multitude of people walk past me toward the escalators or their cars. I saw blacks, whites, Asians, Africans, Indians and Hispanics. I saw couples holding hands. I saw guys with guys and girls with girls. I saw families, mothers and fathers with their kids waving the giant number one hand. I saw a microcosm of the diversity this world contains. It was exciting and shocking, but once I got in the car with my friend and headed to T.G.I.Fridays, I thought nothing else of it.

Later that evening, around one in the morning, I awoke from dream that stays with me as vividly as anything I have ever experienced in my life. I dreamed that night an almost exact version of what I had experienced earlier on Seventh Street NW. It was a dream straight from God.

I dreamed about the man approaching me for money only this time he simply smiled at me and said; "God said feed me!"

The dream continues and as I stand in front of the Gallery Place Metro I watch the multitude stream past me and every last one of them looked at me and said, "God said feed me!" The young Hispanic couple beamed at me and said; "God said feed me!" The African selling scented oils: "God said feed me!" The little boy who carried the big, blue Number 1 hand and tries to run up the side of the wall looked me in my eyes and said; "God said feed me!" White people, black people, men, women and children all speaking in a natural tone of voice, all saying the same thing; "God said feed me!"

I woke up and felt a fire inside of me; burning so deep and so steady. It burns right now as I sit here typing these words. There was/is no doubt in my mind or my spirit as to what the dream meant. I have been called into the ministry as a Shepherd. I have been called to preach the Word of God. To feed God's people. I have answered that call in the affirmative. For those who have been called, know that there isn't any choice in the matter. I am on fire for the Lord and after all He has done for me, I am honored and truly humbled to be called to teach His Word and feed His people.

So, you pray for me. God willing, the next book I write will be authored by Pastor Jonathan Z. Queen. To God be the glory and His will be done.

LOOK AT ME NOW

I'll be honest; I was walking on a path with no promise.
I was on a lonely road, littered with pot holes and lost souls
who had let go of their dreams and forgotten their goals.
Look at me now.
I swear, I wish you could see,
the suffering shadows of those I hurt
standing next to me.
The many lives I've ruined with the games I've played
The totality of my criminality
cannot be measured or weighed,
all because I was afraid… to admit I was afraid.
Look at me now.
Able to admit I've been hurt and I've also caused pain
Able to share my feelings of guilt, resentment and shame,
Knowing I lived a life that was insane
Look at me now.
Can you see that I've changed?
Look at me now and see
A father, a husband, a real man
I think therefore, I am.
I believe therefore, I can.
And I now stand
on the edge of unlimited possibility.
Armed with the attitudes essential
to reaching my full potential.
Look at me now!

On second thought, look at the person to your left,
now to the person on your right,
I'm sure you know the routine
It is a way to display a statistic so obscene.
But recidivism is real and I hate to say it,
the numbers reflect only 1 out of 3 of you will make it.
Well, look at me now!
Believing there is no limit to what I can do.
I will teach you how to be that 1 out of 3
and how to HELP the other 2.
Look at me now!
And please don't mistake my confidence as arrogance,
Or my pride as being proud.
Do not view my assertiveness as being aggressive
Or assume I'm just talking loud,
I simply want you to witness that
I'm walking away from the crowd.
I'm walking away from my self-indulgence,
my fast and easy operations.
I'm letting go of my false image,
my tactics and manipulations.
I'm giving myself options and overcoming
the insanity of my addiction.
I've learned the road to Pro-Social Living
is a lifelong mission.
I've learned that effective communication
requires that I must first listen.
Look at me now!
Making better decisions.
Before I act, I think of the consequences.

I close my eyes and visualize
the hand-cuffs and razor-wire fences.
I picture the faces of my family saddened with despair,
I picture my children with their heads bowed in prayer
As they whisper with deep sorrow
I wish daddy was here.
Look at me now!
I'm not going anywhere!
Look at me now...
Recognizing I still have work to do.
So I close with this reminder for me, and for you
I will stay true.
When the demons from my past come at me,
You know how they do.
When they say: Jonathan Zaki Queen you were a liar,
a drug-dealer, an addict, a drunk.
You were a deadbeat dad, a criminal, a street punk
You were a bad person and your lifestyle was foul
I won't get defensive or let my thoughts get wild.
I won't ball up my fists or give them a mean scowl
I will take a deep breath and try my best to smile
And say, "Yes, I was and I am truly sorry, but please…

Look at me now!

I AM SANE!!!

Acknowledgements

I must first give honor, praise and glory to God. I am so in awe of your mercy and grace. You have truly blessed me even though I remain unworthy. Without you, I am nothing. I thank you for giving me the wisdom, the words and the will to write them and speak them with confidence. I commit my life to teach and exemplify the love of Jesus. I only ask as David asked, *Let the words of my mouth, and the meditation of my heart, be acceptable in your sight, O LORD, my strength, and my redeemer.*

To Lenia, my wife and my soul mate. I could never put into words, how much I appreciate you and everything you do to support what God has ordained for us. Thank you for all of the sacrifices you made in order for me to finally finish this book. From bringing my dinner to me at the computer even though you wanted me at the table; to telling me to "go work on the book" even though there were things that needed done in the house; to reading every word and letting me know when something didn't fit. Thank you for being my partner, best friend and biggest fan. You are my Helpmate and my Virtuous women. I love you, Baby!

To my children, Tramayne, Jonathan II, Jonee, Jazmine, Cheyenne, Mekhi, and Frankie. You remain my strongest motivation to set a new example. I pray that each of you continue to find that beautiful balance of loving who you are, while remaining open to the opportunity of becoming better. I love you and I thank you for helping me grow.

To my mother, Doreen Queen. The greatness you say you see in me is simply a reflection of the greatness in you. Thank you for your forgiveness and for giving me to God even when you had no idea that was the plan. I love you, Mom and I miss you so much. Please do not forget your promise.

To the Queen family, thank you for teaching me loyalty and real love. Despite the dysfunction, we survived and we have a legacy that will continue to become greater with each generation. No matter what I lose or gain, you are the roots of the man I have become. Thank you for loving me and believing in me every time. To my brother, Jaalil and the rest of our 'younger generation' thank you for believing that we can do better and challenging us to do so.

To the Smallwood family, thank you so much for supporting my dreams as if you've known about them your whole lives. Mom Yvette, you are a beautiful example of family love. Dad Doug, thank you for filling one of my voids; for calling me son and meaning it. Doug Jr, your support has been incredible and I look forward to contributing to the success that awaits *you*. To all of you, I am truly blessed to be counted in your family.

I issued many personal acknowledgements in my first book, *Don't Blame Me: The Convict Chronicles* and I would love to do the same here. Unfortunately, I would need another book to thank everyone who has inspired, motivated and encouraged me these past two years.

What I will do here is mention some of the people who were an important part of this project. For everyone else, I will have a running Acknowledgement Board on the Asikari Publishing website, www.asikaripublishing.com. I promise, I will shout you out on there, especially if you remind me.

I want to thank the following people for contributing either their time, money, experience, expertise or influence: Dad, Aunt Gert, Aunt Marva, Lenia, Aunt Bone, Aunt Nette, Aunt Teeny, Jack O, Tony & Trina T, Marcus and DJ Bates, Damali Queen, Shawn Queen, Aunt Karen, Deacon Morrison, Mr. Walker, Reverend Vaughn. Lou 'Lupah Ent' Lambert, Laura Ravenhorst, Jon Parham, Adel Ismail, Len & Derica Wade, Mark L. & Lachanda S., Eric B., Cynthia R., Billy at AA Printing, Sayre Enterprises Inc's Production Plant & Headquarters, Scott and Mary Sayre, Tammy Irvine, Maddie Green, Teresa Downs, Pam M., Pam T., Susan W., First Baptist Church of Lexington, Reverend Shambry, Rev Harris, Rev. McCoy, Rev. Crawley, Pastor D, Pastor TJ, Rev. Glasgow, Shawn 'Frogg' Banks, Malik & Antoinette Aziz, The National Exhoodus Council, Mark Kearney, Poe Cobb, BOP RDAP, Unicor, Nealy at The Urban Word, Rashod and Mike & Suavv Magazine, Rodney, Knia and NY Gospel Magazine, Chuck D & 'On The Real' Radio.

To all of the schools, youth centers, authors, bookstores, book clubs, blogtalk/radio shows, newspapers, magazines and reporters who have shown me love. Thank you!

And a special thank you to the incarcerated men and women who encourage me with their letters and phone calls. I haven't forgotten you. God willing, I will continue to make you proud by making it cool to change for the better and set a new example.

May God bless you and keep you!!!

ABOUT THE AUTHOR

Jonathan Z. Queen, the oldest of five children, was raised in an impoverished neighborhood in Harrisburg, PA by a struggling, single mother. He began using and selling drugs at the age of 14. At the age of 23, he was arrested for the third time, labeled a Career-Criminal and sentenced to 10 years in a Federal Prison.

During the last four years of his 9-year prison sentence, Jonathan completed over 18 months of criminal behavior and drug education programs. He subsequently volunteered for the 500-hour Residential Drug-Abuse Program, where he became a Peer Counselor, Sponsor and Board Member on the Education/ Tutoring Committee. Jonathan graduated first in his RDAP class and has become well-versed in Rational Emotive Behavior Therapy (REBT), ABC's of Rational Self Analysis, Criminal Thinking Errors, Anger Management, Conflict Resolution, Victim Impact and Assertive Communication.

Today, Jonathan Z Queen is an author, motivational speaker, playwright, actor, director, and poet. He is the co-founder of **New Mindz Enterprises** and Vice President of **Asikari Publishing, LLC**. He is a contributor to *The Q Review* and an editor/columnist for *NY Gospel Magazine*. He is an ordained deacon at First Baptist Church of Lexington, VA and works as a Government Contract Manager at Sayre Enterprises Inc. where he also directs the employee GED program. More importantly, he is a devoted husband, faithful father and community leader. He was recently featured in the Federal Prison Industry 2008

Annual Report to Congress in an article entitled *The Power of One Success*.

Jonathan is also a member of *The National Exhoodus Council (NEC)*; a nationwide campaign comprised of formerly incarcerated professionals; all are former members of the criminal/drug/gang culture who now manage community-based organizations in 50 cities. Their motto: *Serving Our Country, After Serving Our Time.*

Jonathan Z. Queen is available for speaking engagements, school assemblies, book signings, interviews, reading group discussions, seminars and workshops.

Contact: info@asikaripublishing.com